CONTENTS

ASSISTANT ENGINEER HANDBOOK

by Sarah Jones

GIGS
IN THE
RECORDING
STUDIO
& BEYOND

SCHIRMER
TRADE
BOOKS

New York / London / Paris / Sydney / Tokyo / Berlin / Copenhagen / Madrid

Schirmer Trade Books
A Division of Music Sales Corporation, New York

Exclusive Distributors:
Music Sales Corporation
257 Park Avenue South, New York, NY 10010 USA
Music Sales Limited
8/9 Frith Street, London W1D 3JB England
Music Sales Pty. Limited
120 Rothschild Street, Rosebery, Sydney, NSW 2018, Australia

Order No. SCH 10136
International Standard Book Number: 0.8256.7296.1

Printed in the United States of America
By Vicks Lithography and Printing Corporation

Library of Congress Cataloging-in-Publication Data

Jones, Sarah, 1970-
    Assistant engineer handbook : gigs in the recording studio and beyond / by Sarah Jones.
        p. cm.
    ISBN 0-8256-7296-1 (pbk. : alk. paper)
    1. Acoustical engineering—Vocational guidance. 2. Sound engineers—Vocational guidance. I. Title.
TA365.J56 2004
781.49—dc22
                                        2004009110

ACKNOWLEDGMENTS

First, I would like to extend a huge thank you to the dozens of incredibly talented and articulate engineers, producers, studio managers, techs, educators, consultants, assistants, and interns who shared their stories and insights for this book. Thanks also to Tom Kenny, George Petersen, and Kevin Becka at *Mix* magazine for their valuable industry insider feedback, and to Mum and Leah for their valuable industry outsider feedback. Thank you, Barbara Schultz, for perfecting my grammar, with style.

I am especially grateful to my editor and champion, Andrea Rotondo, for giving me such an amazing opportunity, and for her unwavering encouragement and support throughout this project.

Most of all, I would like to thank my academic mentors for inspiring me to pursue a "dream" career in music and recording: William Moylan at the University of Massachusetts Lowell, Paul Lehrman at Tufts University, and Ray Novack, music director at Beverly High School, in Beverly, Massachusetts.

Credits
Managing Editor: Andrea M. Rotondo
Copyeditor: Barbara Schultz
Cover Design: Mike Bell
Production Director: Dan Earley
Interior Design: Len Vogler
Publicity Coordinator: Alison M. Wofford
Author's Photographer: Karen Dunn

About the Author

Sarah Jones is Features Editor of *Mix* magazine in Emeryville, California. She's written hundreds of articles about the recording business and has interviewed dozens of top-name engineers and producers. She has degrees in Sound Recording Technology and Music Business from the University of Massachusetts Lowell.

Photo courtesy of Karen Dunn

INTRODUCTION

Why would anyone want to be an audio engineer? Forget the glamorous "show biz" image; the truth is, engineering is a hard job. Whether you're working in music, sound-for-picture, live sound, or some other aspect of audio production, you have to start at the bottom, and the story of an assistant engineer is always the same: The pay is dirt…and that's if you're lucky. You're guaranteed to be working with fragile—and gigantic—egos, under difficult, often stressful, conditions. The hours are unpredictable and almost always ridiculously long. You live on caffeine and take-out. There will probably be long stretches when you don't see the light of day. So what's the payoff, then? As an assistant, you'll get to learn the trade in a dynamic, creative environment. And you won't be an assistant forever; at some point, you'll get to exercise your own creativity and make decisions. And no matter what your role is in the studio, the pluses are many: It's an artistic atmosphere, you'll work with some incredibly talented and fascinating people, and you're free from the dreaded nine-to-five daily office grind: Your "cubicle" is a recording studio, a movie set, a concert hall. All that, and you'll have the satisfaction of knowing that you are part of the strong, passionate team creating a quality end result—whether you've produced a demo CD for a local band, nailed the perfect hook for a TV commercial, or pulled off a great-sounding music festival without a hitch. In this book, you'll find the truth about making a go of it in music and audio production: The dues you'll pay and the considerable rewards to be gained.

The classic image of the audio engineer as the "guy behind the glass," kicking back in luxurious recording sessions, spending weeks or months on end hanging out with cool rock stars, was never that true to begin with, and today it's downright unrealistic. However, there are job prospects in more audio fields today than ever before, from Website design to videogame sound to corporate A/V to working for the FBI—and yes, even recording rock stars. There's also a new studio economy: Advancements in low-cost technology create opportunities for more people to build their own professional studios; more and more, top producers and engineers—and even artists—are completing much of their production in their own spaces. In fact, there are plenty of people who work in other fields by day, and produce their own music or paid commercial projects in their home studios, at night and on weekends.

At the same time, the music industry has been taking financial hits, and the excessive recording budgets of the '70s and '80s are history. Those elite studios that built their businesses hosting months-long projects with legendary pop artists are seeing less of their famous clientele, as many artists are spending more time recording in lavishly outfitted "home" studios, and booking minimal time at a public studio at the end of their project to mix. As conventional studios downsize and diversify to stay in business, relying more on freelance staff for everything from mixdown to maintenance, the role of the engineer is adapting and expanding. Technology changes the game, too: Today successful engineers need to be as conversant in file formats, networks, and operating systems as they are in tape alignment. But as much as technology has evolved, core skills remain important: Mic placement skills are as crucial as ever, acoustical principles never change, and the art of communication is timeless. This industry melds art, technology, and commerce, and renders them inseparable.

Success, for some people, is defined by money. For others, success equals job satisfaction. It's important to know where your career priorities lie, because the first and biggest reality check in your audio career will probably be your pay—or lack thereof. This is one profession where you'll find salaries are rarely commensurate with education and experience, especially at the assistant level. Your buddy who just graduated with a degree in accounting might reasonably expect to enter the workforce with a high five-figure salary, great benefits, three weeks of vacation, and a healthy retirement plan. You, on the other hand, can take your degree (or certificate, diploma, or experience) in recording and hope it will allow you a foot in the door at some reputable recording studio, post house, or other production facility to perform menial chores for maybe minimum wage, maybe $10 an hour, maybe nothing at all except for an opportunity to learn about your craft.

However, this can be a highly rewarding business. As an audio engineer, you're actually getting paid to do something that a lot of people would do for free (and far too many people actually do this gig for nothing!). This job is a labor of love, and it's not for everybody. But how many people can truly say they enjoy what they do? Think about it—you spend a huge chunk of your waking hours at work. If that time is enjoyable and fulfilling to you, think how much richer your life will be. You can be one of those lucky ones, if you have the talent, skills, and perseverance.

Before you commit to a life in recording, you should be 100% sure this is your calling. Do your homework so you can move forward armed with realistic expectations about both your career path and the industry in general. Understand the realities of this vocation. Be comfortable with long hours, low pay, and limited upward mobility. Realize that it's going to be a difficult journey and the rewards will likely be a long time coming. Do some soul searching.

This book will tell you what you need to know to get started on your quest. You'll get advice from those who have made it to the top, those still working toward their big break, and even parting tips from those who have left to pursue other fields. You'll learn what many of them wish somebody had told them when they were just starting out. And equipped with that knowledge, you'll have the tools you need to set out on your career. But implementing them is up to you. Nobody is going to hand you a job. In the audio industry, there's no one "right" way to build your career. People have found success through wildly different journeys, from going through audio educational programs and internships to working their way up on the job, to relying on networking and sheer luck. But only you will be able to determine which path is best for you, and for that, self-assuredness is key: In this industry without rules, sometimes the only constants that you can count on are your own skills, personality, work ethic, and ability to sell yourself.

So, why would anyone want this job? We do it because we have to. It's in our blood. We can't do anything else. We know that magic happens when we drop our favorite CD into the changer, or when our stadium seat rumbles during the climax of an action movie, or when we hear—and *feel*—the first chord rip through the arena. We want to be a part of that world. It's a dream job, and we want the satisfaction of knowing we are going to work every day to do something we love. Are you still in? Read on.

CHAPTER ONE

ASSISTANT ENGINEERING 101

So what's this job all about, anyway? Well, first let's take a look at what it isn't. It isn't what you see in movies, and it's definitely not what you watch on MTV. A lot of people in recording studios are often depicted as livin' the rock-star lifestyle. Imagine lavish major-label projects with massive budgets. Megastars with stretch limos and huge entourages taking over mega multiroom studios. Endless parties. You hear epic tales from veteran studio engineers who worked hard and played harder, slowly inching their way up, scrubbing toilets for the privilege of lounging in the studio with rock stars for months on end. Well, if you think this job is all about partying, you're in for a big shock.

No matter which slice of the industry you look at, whether in live sound, film, TV/radio broadcast—or even, yes, the music studio—there's a lot of hard work being done by serious professionals. With the development of both technology and educational programs, audio engineering has evolved into a "real" career. And studio jobs are just the tip of the iceberg (which is a good thing, since there are only about 50 major U.S. recording studios and thousands of new recording school grads hitting the market each year). There are endless career opportunities in audio, in some surprising places. Think about the sounds you hear everywhere around you: Your cell phone ringer. The power-up tones on your computer. The "door is open" and "lights on" alerts in your car. The song you hear when you open a musical greeting card. Those 911 call playbacks on "Cops." The effects you hear on an amusement park ride. All of these were produced by an audio engineer, and that engineer could someday be you.

There's a lot of mystique surrounding recording. Most people have no idea what happens between when an artist first performs a song or an actor reads lines, and the end result: A CD, movie, or concert. It's fun to talk about this job—it makes you look great at high school reunions and family Christmas gatherings, and all your friends talk about what an incredible, glamorous job you have. But behind the glass, or backstage, it's very different. The reality is, audio engineering is a lot of hard work. It can be tedious and repetitive—even the "recording rock stars" part. It's not unusual to spend days laboring over one song in the studio, or capturing one scene on a movie set. You can't choose the hours, and they can be unpredictable. In most areas of audio production, this is not a nine-to-five desk job. In fact, you probably won't have an office or a "desk," except for the console in the studio.

"You'd have to be nuts to get into this industry because you think it's this glamorous, rock & roll life. You'll be in for a lot of disappointment," says studio designer and speaker developer Chris Pelonis. "I remember when I was making a record years ago, and I've got a friend who's a maniac; life is just a party to this guy. He wanted to come down to the studio. He shows up with a case of beer, and I'm working on the same two bars for three-and-a-half hours. After about half an hour, he said, 'God, is this really what it's like?' And I said, 'No, it's like this, plus another ten hours. We're not even close to getting this.' He said, 'Well, do we get to eat dinner?' And I said, 'Probably around midnight we'll take a break for dinner.' 'Are we going to go to some bars or something? Aren't there, like, girls that hang around for this stuff?' I said, 'Well, not usually, unless they're singing.' Of course, the other side to that is, if you turn out to be in a band like Aerosmith or something, I think that that's everything that you think it is, and then some. I don't think there's any surprises. But to be behind the scenes, it is what you make of it."

In this chapter, as I talk about the skills you'll need to become an audio engineer and your career options, I'll be throwing a lot of information at you. You may feel overwhelmed, but take all this in stride. There's a broad skill set here, but there's also a huge range of jobs defined and not every skill is necessary for each job. As you discover what your interests are and narrow your focus, you'll determine which skills are most essential for you.

Engineering, Defined

An audio engineer, by definition, is responsible for capturing, manipulating, and replicating sound. There are many variations of this job, from mixing rock albums to designing movie sound effects to analyzing crime scene clues, but they all boil down to operating equipment involved in playing, mixing, or recording audio. The goal of the audio engineer is to technically translate the artistic vision of the producer, the artist, or the director.

A great performance and great sound are two different concepts. Think of a time when you enjoyed a performance, but the sound was terrible. Maybe you listened to a great old archive of blues recordings, but the audio was so distorted you could barely make out what the singer was saying. Perhaps it was a concert that was so loud that you thought your ears might bleed. Or maybe you were watching a tearjerker season finale on a TV drama but were distracted because the dying girlfriend's dialog didn't quite match up with her moving lips. That's the difference, and that's where the engineer comes in: Although the entire production team works to facilitate the best performance from an artist, the engineer's goal is to capture the best sonic quality of that performance.

Legendary engineer Bruce Swedien, who's spent the past 40 years recording everyone from Count Basie, Duke Ellington, and Quincy Jones to Michael Jackson, Mick Jagger, and Jennifer Lopez, stresses the importance of understanding how something sounds before adding your own sonic imprint. "I think one of the biggest mistakes perhaps a lot of young people make is to try to record music by listening to people's recordings," he says. "It's the worst mistake you can make. I truly believe that the only way to learn to make meaningful recordings is to know what music sounds like. If you're going to record music, you've got to go out and listen to live music in a good acoustical situation and develop a benchmark with your ear that has at its core reality in sound. Once you know what music sounds like in an acoustic situation, then you can go crazy in the studio. You can break all the rules and do things to make your own sonic statement."

The term "engineer" can mean a lot of things. Some people who are considered top engineers may know next to nothing about technology, but they have incredible ears. They make good decisions about balance and depth, or which compressor to use, but they might not have a clue as to what a compressor actually does—they just know what it sounds like. Sometimes those people might be considered producers who push faders. This is not to say they aren't true professionals; some top engineers are much more focused on the artistic side than the tech side; others are more immersed in the technology. You'll encounter many classes of engineers, at every industry level.

In a recording studio, an engineer's job is multifaceted. He or she plans and executes the technical aspect of recording sessions (sometimes working with the producer), selects and configures microphones and effects equipment, sets up the performers, and records to tape or a digital audio workstation. An engineer also edits the recording, makes duplicate copies, and archives. These days, the role of the assistant (or second) engineer is even harder to define. Generally, a recording studio assistant helps set up equipment, such as mics and cables, documents session information, and operates a recorder, which may be a tape machine or a workstation. The assistant usually acts as a gofer for the session, replacing headphones and cables, and performing other chores as needed. Assistant engineers are often responsible for maintenance tasks like documenting, stocking, and ordering inventory; repairing cables and headphones; and keeping the studio organized and clean.

The type of person who is drawn to this field is multitalented. A successful engineer is both creative and technically savvy. He or she needs to know how everything works, has a passion for music, great ears, and is diplomatic, easy going, a multitasker, and good at troubleshooting to boot.

As far as recording studio jobs are concerned, the music industry has gone through an upheaval in recent years, creating a new working environment today. When recording studios were operated by major record labels with huge budgets, they employed large staffs of engineers. These days, you're likely to encounter a lot more freelance and independent engineers. (And often, they have their *own* assistants.) Why? The advent of cheaper, more powerful digital technology has diminished the need for large recording consoles—one of the major draws of large facilities, along with large tracking spaces and hot gear lists—and spawned the growth of home studios and midrange commercial studios. Often, major artists save the big studios for mixing, doing the bulk of preproduction in high-end "home" studios beforehand. As a result, many studios have seen a decline in business and have cut staff to stay afloat. As studios downsize their staffs, relying more on project-by-project contract work, the number of freelance engineers continues to rise.

Now, people with just a few thousand dollars' worth of gear are producing professional material in midrange or even home studios. A rack full of hot gear, however, doesn't necessarily equal a hit record. "Today, musicians are led to believe by software and hardware manufacturers that they don't need an engineer or producer or commercial recording studio; all they need is gear," says Berklee College of Music professor Stephen Webber. "There is an obvious financial incentive for musicians to try to do it on their own, as well. Therefore, people entering the field today must possess a lot of obvious tangible and quantifiable skill. It needs to be apparent to the artist almost immediately that things go faster and better with a professional producer and engineer. If you can't deliver to your client the feeling that things are sounding much better than they ever would have sounded without your involvement, there is no reason for you to be there."

Both freelance and staff engineer responsibilities are evolving with this shift in structure, but the basic philosophy of the assistant engineer is the same: Your job is to help the producer (or front-of-house mixer, or location recordist) implement the vision of an artist.

CHANGING TECHNOLOGIES MEAN NEW SKILLS

In every aspect of the audio industry, from music to live sound to film, new technologies mean new skills are needed. In addition to mastering soldering and mic placement techniques, today an engineer must be able to encode files, defragment drives, fix software glitches, even troubleshoot a network.

Everyone agrees, workstation fluency is essential. "Whether it's Pro Tools, Nuendo, Logic, or another platform, you need to be able to get around on an audio workstation nowadays," says Nell Thompson, of Full Sail Real World Education. "They're a standard tool of the trade, whereas ten years ago they were far less common due to cost, compatibility, and reliability issues." These days, you have to not only be fluent on many platforms, but understand how all the components work together. You must be aware of upgrades and compatibility issues among computers, software, and interfaces, and be able to keep them all talking to each other. "Just as important as knowing how they work is knowing how they *don't* work; that is, how to prevent and/or overcome things going wrong, like machine crashes and failures, corrupted or lost files, MIDI interruptions, or sync problems," says Tufts University professor Paul Lehrman. "Having an excellent overall knowledge of the computer you're on—Mac or Wintel or whatever—and its operating system is essential." It used to be that there weren't many pieces of gear to update, and engineers would often rely on techs to take care of that task. Nowadays, gear that you had running smoothly last week may not be working at all this week, because you installed a new operating system or a new plug-in. At the very least, if you don't know how to fix these problems yourself, you have to know whom to call.

Production sound mixer Arthur Rochester, who has been nominated for multiple Academy Awards for his work on such films as *The Conversation*, *Con Air*, and *Master and Commande*r, says that new, improved technologies have brought some consolidation of tasks, but he's not sure if anyone's actually saving any time as a result. "Because the DAW operator has his or her hands full doing all those jobs, there is still other work to be done," he says. "It is necessary to see the rehearsals with the actors or musicians. The studio needs to be set up for the session or scene. Microphones have to be set up and cables run, or radio mics have to be set on the actors; levels have to be set. There is not an end to work just because the recording medium has changed. There are still jobs that demand the same degree of attention to detail. There are tasks 'outside the box' that must be accomplished. Advances in technology offer us more tools with which to work in addition to more time and freedom to create."

Engineer and professor Noel Smith, who develops the curriculum at New York's Institute of Audio Research, says that years ago, when he worked as a musician, the engineer's position was more clearly defined. "I always knew what the role of the engineer was. I knew that there were two people in the control room: The person who knew about music, and the guy with the pocket protector, who may or may not have known about music, but that wasn't his 'job,'" he says. "So I always knew there was a distinction among the three of us: I played, the producer made a judgment, the engineer did what the engineer was supposed to do. That's no longer the case anymore. Music engineering is almost nonexistent. It is so blurred between producing and playing the non-real instruments that it's very hard to see where engineering actually is, versus where production and creation is."

Miami studio engineer/Pro Tools instructor Mihai Boloni agrees that his role as an engineer has expanded radically with advances in audio technology: "This past year has been an interesting time for me; I've been thrust into this role where I do just as much production as engineering," he says. "I by no means consider myself a producer. But I've had to learn music theory. I've had to learn every synthesizer on the planet, how they work; MIDI is a huge part. Oftentimes, I'll wind up doing production as much as I do engineering."

At the same time, Boloni says, it's hard to tell whether powerful computer applications will ultimately add duties to the engineer's job description, or create new niche roles: "The technology is enabling us to do more and more things on a daily basis," he says. "I remember with Pro Tools 3, MIDI was basically nonexistent. But as technology evolves, computers have gotten more powerful, software's gotten more powerful. Are we going to see a MIDI guy who doesn't know anything else, and an audio guy who doesn't know anything about MIDI? Or are we going to homogenize the two into this end-all be-all production person? I think for a lot of studios, that's really the case; they'd rather pay one guy a little more money because he can do everything, instead of having to farm out work to three different people who might not be in communication with one another. With software getting as powerful as it is now, one person can take an artist or producer from scratch to the final product."

With all this talk of technology, it's important to remember that the core qualities that make a great recording engineer are timeless. "Some of the new skills needed include adaptability to changing technology, openness to varied musical genres, knowledge of related technologies like networking, video production, and computer science," says Middle Tennessee State University Recording Industry department chairman Chris Haseleu. "However, the 'old' skills of being able to communicate, work in a high-pressure environment, have good microphone techniques, and be able to produce a balanced mix are still central to being a good engineer."

An Educational Evolution

Twenty years ago, an audio engineer's schooling meant learning by the seat of his pants through apprentice-based on-the-job training. The phrase "audio education" was an oxymoron. But we're witnessing the end of that era, as complex technology requires more sophisticated skills, and schools continue to develop superior recording programs. Audio as a discipline has certainly become less a "trade" and more a "profession." Opportunities for learning the ropes on the job still exist, but it's becoming increasingly difficult to progress very far without any kind of formal education. (I'll go into this topic in depth, in Chapter Two, Your Game Plan.) "I think employers prefer applicants with a real education, since that usually means they'll have a broader background, and be more flexible within the organization," says Paul Lehrman. "Someone who has just mixed electronic music and doesn't know anything about microphones is going to be less valuable than someone who has studied polar patterns, grounding issues, etc., no matter how great a mixer he or she might be."

"I think an education is pretty much required nowadays, if for no other reason than there are plenty of schools producing graduates who can fill the open positions," adds MTSU's Chris Haseleu. "That does not mean that folks just starting out will not have to spend some time 'learning the ropes' in an internship or similar position. One of the things the good schools do is to teach the students how to learn and adapt to the differing technologies and work environments found in the different parts of the industry."

This story is the same, no matter which area of the industry you pursue. Live sound engineer Robert Scovill, who's toured with the likes of Tom Petty, Matchbox 20, Prince, and Def Leppard, says that back when he was just starting out a couple of decades ago, it was easier to concentrate more on the fundamentals of sound, because the equipment was relatively simple to operate. "Now, you need a couple of years of schooling just to get a handle on the technology," he says. "It's very difficult now to be the motorcycle mechanic and walk into a sound company and say, 'Can I get a gig?' and have it parlay into anything of worth, because the learning curve is so steep. You can't be one of the buddies of the band who knows a lot about stereos and get a gig anymore. It's a different world out there."

Leslie Ann Jones, director of Skywalker Sound's scoring stage, adds that in today's economic climate, facilities simply don't have the luxury of taking the time to teach new hires the ropes. "In the old days—which was only just a couple of years ago—many of us didn't want to hire somebody from school," she says. "We wanted to be able to kind of mold people the way we wanted. But the problem is, there aren't that many multifroom facilities anymore that can actually spend the time training someone."

A Long List of Skills

You don't have to learn much to make a record, but to make a *good* record takes talent and skill. Okay, a whole bunch of skills. The same goes for live sound or post-production. Making something happen and making it happen really well are two different things. As an engineer, you're in the unlikely position of using technical expertise to realize artistic ideas. How do you build a song to a climax? How do you make the guitar "pop" in the mix? How do you use sound to grab the audience's attention onscreen? Whether you're on tour, in the studio, or on the set, you'll constantly juggle your scientific knowledge, your musical intuition, your audio expertise, and your political savvy to make the session work. Let's take a look at a few of the skills you'll need to become a successful audio engineer. I'm going to bombard you here, but don't worry, you can do it!

Math and Science

−20 dBfs = 0 VU = +4 dBU = 85 dB SPL. What the hell does that mean? Do you feel like you're staring at hieroglyphics? There are two things you should know here: One, it's not as complicated as you think. Two, get over it! This industry is a marriage of art and technology. If you're going to make it as an audio engineer, you'll not only have to be a creative genius, but you'll need a basic aptitude for science. We're not talking about conquering quantum mechanics here, just having a handle on simple mathematics, the principles of sound, and electronics basics.

It's important to understand acoustic concepts. What makes your voice sound different from a flute, which sounds nothing like an electric guitar? Why does a musical performance sound different in an empty concert hall from the way it sounds in a full one? How does sound emanate from a cello? Why do the mixes you've done in your bedroom sound great in your bedroom, but not in other places? Why does the same CD sound completely different in your living room, in your car, and through your headphones? And why don't we all sound as fabulous all the time as when we sing in the shower? You'll need to understand the basic physics of sound, including the behavior of sound waves and acoustical properties of structures, spaces, and materials, and how things like your walls, ceiling, and floor interact with your speakers.

Music

It's easy to draw parallels between music and audio production. Audio is, after all, organized sound, and so is music. Learning music gives you an understanding of pitch and timbre, how sounds emanate from instruments, and how instruments or voices fit in an arrangement. If you know the range of a saxophone, for example, it will help you to determine why that sax solo is getting buried onstage, and how to bring it out in the mix. Or say you're tracking a barbershop quartet, and one of the voices is standing out too much. With a little musical training, it will be easier to determine whether one voice is actually projecting too loud—and which voice it is—or if the problem lies in the mic setup, and whether adding or subtracting bands of EQ will solve the problem. Perhaps you're mixing film effects and dialog; understanding timbre can help you know how to make sure the spoken lines can be clearly understood over the footsteps.

Musical ability is certainly not crucial in every situation, but it does help to be able to speak the language of musicians. If you're a musician, develop your skills. Consider learning some theory. Being able to follow along with a piece of music can really boost your value in a session, whether the producer wants you to "punch in the guitar in bar three of the second verse" or "edit out that flat third sixteenth-note *pizzicato* f-sharp in measure nine of the second viola part."

Maybe you're not a musician. You still might want to think about taking a few piano or guitar lessons. You'll learn about basic harmony, and you'll have the side benefit of impressing your friends at parties with your rock & roll skills. Having some kind of facility on an instrument or with your voice can also help you anticipate musicians' needs. You'll know, for example, why you shouldn't offer a singer a glass of milk before a session, or why you need to stop a session so that the guitarist can change a string, rather than just tossing her another axe. If you play with an ensemble, you'll understand why the members of that jazz combo in the tracking room need to be able to see each other while they play. If you get onstage, you'll understand the importance of the perfect monitor mix.

Kevin Becka, an engineer who serves as associate director of education at the

Conservatory of Recording Arts (near Phoenix) says his music background has always been an asset for him in the studio. "I was in a situation working with a really big guitar player, a great guy, who came up as a player—not because he was well-schooled, but because he could play his ass off," he says. "In one session, we were doing overdubs on a project for a Japanese client, and he was trying to write a chart and figure out one chord. I have a really good set of ears, and this one change came up, and he was having a hard time figuring it out; and I just said, 'I think that's a D7+9.' In that case, I was able to help out. Also, to give players cues, you have to speak that language. If they say, 'I want to go back to that bridge,' I can rewind and say, 'I'll give you two bars.' I was writing charts, I knew song structure, so I could communicate easily as a musician."

Playing an instrument or singing will teach you that performing is a physical task, with limitations, and you'll be more conscious of the players' endurance levels in the studio. Singing or playing an acoustic instrument also helps increase your awareness of a performance space, whether you're recording a string ensemble in a church, mixing a rock band at a local club, or capturing "room sound" on a movie set. You've got to have enough sense of pitch to know when a track is in tune, and musical knowledge helps in this area.

Electronics

As far as electronics is concerned, you should have a familiarity with basic concepts so you understand how equipment works. You'll need to know what phantom power is, what grounding means, and how balanced power works, and you should be fluent enough to be able to both troubleshoot problem gear and avoid common issues, such as jitter, noise, hum, and other electrical problems that can plague an audio signal.

Here's a scenario: You're in the studio with a big producer and a hot, up-and-coming, heavy-metal band. You're getting ready to track the session, and as the guitarist is warming up, you hear a nasty buzzing noise. The producer turns to you and grumbles, "We need to get rid of that @#%!& 60-cycle hum." What do you do? Well, it helps if you know what 60-cycle hum sounds like, where it's coming from, and most importantly, how to get rid of it. (For a solid, no-nonsense education in audio electronics, pick up Patrick L. McKeen's book, *Keep Your Gear Running: Electronics for Musicians*.)

Signal Flow

It's crucial to understand signal flow and what happens to sound during the recording process. When you sing into a microphone, how does it pick up the sound of your voice? What happens to sound between the mic and speakers? Your audio signal might pass through a lot of gear along the way. What happens when it passes through a recording console and effects gear? You need to be able to understand how an equalizer works, what a compression curve is, what these processes do to your signal. You also need to be able to troubleshoot: What do you do if you sing into the mic and nothing happens? Know how to walk through the signal chain to isolate the problem, versus blindly swapping out mics, cables, and gear.

What happens when you perform the same processes within a computer workstation? In other words, what happens when digital audio, which is ultimately just data, is manipulated? You must grasp the mathematics of digital technology: Why can you only fit about 76 minutes of CD-quality audio on a compact disc, but the same disc can hold hundreds of MP3s? What happens during MP3 encoding that allows the file to be so small, and how does it affect what you're hearing? What is lossy versus lossless compression? A lot of this is basic math.

It's a given that in order to succeed in any industry today, you're going to need strong computer skills, both in hardware platforms and common business applications, such as Microsoft Word and Excel. In our business, however, you'll have to be proficient in a workstation platform. (Digidesign Pro Tools is the most widely used.) You'll also need to know your way around a variety of audio plug-in applications, and understand how various operating systems affect those applications, and how they affect each other, in addition to how they manipulate your sounds.

"Without a doubt, the computer has altered the studio more than anything," says William Moylan, chairperson of the Department of Music and coordinator of the Sound Recording Technology program at the University of Massachusetts Lowell. "There was once a time when an engineer did not encounter a computer in the entire signal chain. Now, nearly the entire signal chain can be contained within a single computer. So, computer skills are a must, along with a secure knowledge of what data stream is under consideration at any time."

Web Skills

You're probably sick of the cliché "global economy," but it's true. The Internet has really leveled the playing field in a lot of areas of the music business: With online distribution of music, you can put a song up on the Web, and it can be heard around the world in a matter of minutes. The Web has created new niche opportunities in every aspect of the audio business. Engineers who master new media apps are creating sound for Websites. Studios are adding services such as Web encoding and delivery of their projects. Concerts are being "Webcast" in real time. Engineers are even collaborating internationally on projects over the Internet. With all of these opportunities come new skill requirements, such as understanding codecs, programming HTML, and authoring in multimedia applications such as QuickTime and Flash.

Human Hearing

Feeling well-rounded yet? Wait, there's more. To do this job, you also need to understand how humans hear, which involves a lot of physiology, plus a little psychology. For example: When someone calls your name in a crowd, how do you know which way to turn? Why do you sometimes swear you hear your phone ringing while you're playing a CD, only to be surprised when you're wrong? What does it mean if your ears ring after a rock concert? Why does pressing the "loudness" button make your tiny boombox suddenly sound like it's attached to a big subwoofer?

Communication

"In audio production and filmmaking, it's not one person and your art; it's not 'me, my canvas, and my oils, and I'm painting by myself,'" says David Leonard, founder and CEO of the Trebas Institute in Montreal and Toronto. "You're working with a team of people, so communication is essential." It doesn't matter if you have the best engineering chops in the world if you can't express yourself clearly to the people around you, whether they're the talent in the studio, the producer, the producer's girlfriend, or the pizza delivery guy. And if you want to be a producer some day, that job is all about communication.

Having good instincts about how to handle various scenarios is also key. "Every situation has a protocol and certain expectations from all of the participants," says Berklee's Stephen Webber. "People who are able to quickly size up a situation, how they fit in, and how they can best add value are going to do well. Perception skills are not as easy to teach as more factual material, but aptitude in this area probably has more to do with a person's ultimate success."

Your job as an engineer also includes doing everything you can to build up an artist's confidence, onstage, in a session, or on location. "'Emotional massage' is the best term I've heard for it," says Kevin Becka. "It's a win-win situation: They'll be more comfortable, and you'll get a better track. That's the cool part for me—being able to convince people that they can be a lot better than they think they can."

Ears!

Above all, a top engineer has to have great ears. Are you capable of critical listening? You've probably heard the phrase "golden ears." The most successful engineers in this business have highly sophisticated listening skills (which are often more relevant than their technical chops), a combination of fortunate genetics and careful cultivation over time. Their ears are sensitive to the most minute changes in pitch, volume, panning, and other aspects of a mix. They are exceedingly attuned to the acoustic properties of their working environment. (They could be compared to connoisseurs who can break down the complex flavors in fine wines.) Don't be overwhelmed by this concept, however. Though there's much to be said for natural talent here; with practice, you can train your ears to detect changes as subtle as a few decibels in loudness, a few milliseconds of reverb time, or a few frames of sync offset.

Having great ears also means being able to listen objectivity. IAR's Noel Smith says listening is the most important skill he teaches his students. "There are lots of different issues about good-quality sound and bad-quality sound, and it's all very subjective," he says. "A distorted guitar sound, to someone who was an engineer in the '50s, or a designer, or a musician, would have been a no-no. But that very same distorted guitar is probably the iconic sound of rock music. It is distorted and that's good, not necessarily bad. So the issue is not about judging whether it is right or wrong, but recognizing it for what it is. And in order to do that, you really have to develop a sense of hearing. I don't mean to say the 'golden ears' kind of thing, because I think that's a gift that you really hone—golden ears certainly help—but most students are capable of sharpening their listening skills and their understanding of what they're listening to; how they're perceiving it."

Well, that's quite a skills checklist. This may all seem overwhelming, but let's face it: A monkey can learn to turn knobs and push faders. And it's important to remember that, although it's crucial to master all the tools, in the end, it still boils down to your talent and creativity. Producer/engineer Jimmy Douglass sums it up best: "Tools are not going to save you, they're only going to enhance what you can already do on your own."

Skills Checklist
A great audio engineer has a command of:

- ☐ Math
- ☐ Acoustics
- ☐ Music Theory & Concepts
- ☐ Electronics
- ☐ Signal Flow
- ☐ Troubleshooting
- ☐ Computer Skills
- ☐ Web Programming
- ☐ Hearing Physiology
- ☐ Business
- ☐ Communication
- ☐ Professionalism
- ☐ Critical Listening
- ☐ Patience

OPPORTUNITIES IN A COMPETITIVE FIELD

Most people who have been around the business a long time agree that the decision to work in this industry shouldn't be taken lightly. "I don't think any career in audio is for the wimpy," says Chris Pelonis. "You gotta be ready to kick ass and work ridiculous hours and really sacrifice for it."

"The reality is, for every engineering job there are a hundred assistants who want it. For every assistant job, there are a hundred interns who want it," adds Bill Ring, chief maintenance tech at New York's Quad Recording, which has hosted the likes of the Rolling Stones, U2, Madonna, OutKast, Garth Brooks, Stevie Wonder, Coldplay, and Jay-Z. He admits he's exaggerating, but he doesn't seem that far off the mark. Although there are more job opportunities in our industry today than ever before, there are even more talented—and highly motivated—job hunters seeking them out. So make sure you're ready to do what it takes to make it. "Don't consider this career unless you know this is why you were put on the earth," says Stephen Webber. "The people you will be competing with will be that driven, and if you are not, you are not likely to succeed."

With all the "big name" glitz and glamour of the recording business, it's easy to forget that the world of audio production is really a cottage industry and that studios are, for the most part, mom-and-pop shops. There are no policies for hiring practices, no prerequisite experience requirements, no salary regulations, or benefit standards. Studio engineers might make $15 an hour, or they can make thousands of dollars a day, or nothing at all. In other words, there are no rules. The same is true in live sound. Exceptions can be found in areas like post-production, broadcast, theater, and other fields where union work is the norm. There, salaries, hours, and job parameters are set and regulated by union groups. Other areas that offer more "traditional" employment benefits include corporate A/V, "special venue" (i.e. amusement park) audio production, and equipment manufacturing.

BEYOND THE STUDIO GIG

These days, there are more opportunities than ever, in a wide variety of fields from multimedia production to forensic analysis. If your sole dream is to make records for rock stars, then you're missing out on some really creative and rewarding careers in audio.

When people think of an audio engineer, they usually envision someone sitting behind a console in a recording studio, pushing faders while a rock band plays. Yes, that picture is real. But the truth is, there are dozens of audio career options in a wide variety of fields, from film, television, and theater sound, to game design, to education, to journalism. Corporations such as Coca-Cola, FedEx, General Motors, the NFL, and Boeing have in-house studios. The FBI and NASA have audio engineers. You can make a living producing cell-phone ring tones. Let's take a look at career options, traditional ones and those in places you'd never expect.

Music Recording

The most popular audio vocation is music recording. Music is universal, and there's a lot of it being made. This is a high-profile field, and many audio engineering jobs fall under this category.

In terms of recording pop music (for the sake of argument here, anything that isn't classical music), whether that's cutting an album with a local band or a Top 40 artist, the engineer's role is the same: Find a way to use technology to implement the artistic vision of the producer, who directs the session.

The "traditional" role of studio engineer can take many forms. It used to be that recording engineers were staff employees at record labels and recording studios, and that is still true in some cases. But today we're seeing more and more freelance engineers, or engineers who run their own project studios. Freelance engineers may be high profile, with solid reputations, and a lot of experience under their belts.

They can be in demand by many studios and clients, and some top artists work exclusively with them. Freelance engineers may even bring in their own assistants and interns.

On the other hand, many studios still employ their own engineers, sometimes contracting extra help for major projects. The pluses of being a staff engineer are many. There's a lot of comfort in having a stable, steady gig, especially if benefits are involved. Working full time at a facility allows you to gain experience working on a variety of projects in a familiar setting, while building your network. At many music facilities, including most project studios and smaller commercial facilities, the same person performs both recording and mixing engineering duties. However, at some larger production facilities (and in the case of many high-profile freelancers), it's more common to encounter specialized recording engineers who are responsible for selecting microphones, setting up the recording environment, and capturing the performance; and mixing engineers, who balance and fine-tune tracks, combine layers and add effects, to create the mix.

Engineers who record classical music require a slightly different set of skills. Unlike pop music, which is usually "built" in the studio, track by track, classical sessions usually involve recording the entire ensemble, either on location in a concert hall, or in a studio or soundstage. Often, material is spliced together from multiple performances to create a single piece of music. It's not uncommon for a recording of a classical "performance" to contain a few hundred edits, and for this an engineer needs to be able to both follow a music score, and be fast and fluent in computer workstation editing.

Skywalker Sound's Leslie Ann Jones has strong, specific educational requirements for the people she hires. "These days, although I don't look for people often, I do look for people who have more of a depth of experience, as opposed to more contemporary experience. I also look for somebody who knows music in some form or another. This is not the kind of place where we get a lot of hard-rock guitar bands; we all read music here, and we can all follow a score, and much of our work is referenced to notes in the score, things like that, as opposed to verses and choruses."

A mastering engineer performs finishing touches on an album in preparation for duplication. After the recording engineer finishes tracking and mixing, a mastering engineer uses EQ and other effects to make sure all of the final tracks on the recording are at consistent volume and have a similar sonic "feel," the fades between songs are even, etc.

Remixers, or beat-makers, use technology to build new song arrangements from finished pre-existing tracks and samples, adding rhythm tracks and effects to build a new mix of a song, or an entirely new song. They're the people creating most of the dance music on the market. Many remixers work at home, since most of their work is done with electronic instruments and computers, so they don't need a big tracking space or a lot of fancy recording gear. In the hip-hop world, this professional is often referred to as a producer.

Other opportunities for music recording engineers include equipment specialization, on gear such as Pro Tools, Auto-Tune software, and MIDI programming.

Although most engineers are expected to be able to perform basic repairs such as soldering cables and headphones, maintenance techs handle more complex tasks such as large wiring jobs, console channel strip replacement, and speaker driver repair. Quad Recording's chief tech, Bill Ring, says that as a staff engineer, he spends most of his time repairing cables and basic electronics and replacing speakers, but his most important role is to keep sessions on line. "People who want to do tech stuff and are any good at it are comparatively rare," says Ring, "because people who are intelligent and interested in this stuff usually want to be the glamour guy, the engineer, because it's much more glamorous to be the person who mixes the album than it is to be the person lying under the console like a garage mechanic with a flashlight in your teeth." Even if you don't want to be a tech, it's very important to master the basics and become a proficient troubleshooter since many studios can't afford to pay a full-time tech. If something goes wrong during your session, you're the one who has to save the day.

Sound Reinforcement

Live sound involves sound design and reinforcement for performances and special events—everything from rock concerts to the SuperBowl to Broadway theater, and anywhere from 35,000-seat arenas to the local bar or club. Here, the mixer's job is to interpret and deliver the sound to a live audience, whether that sound is a musical performance, sports event, or a public speech.

Live sound engineers often deal with different venues and different people every night, so in addition to having audio chops, they need to be quick on their feet, flexible, and great problem-solvers. "Sound reinforcement requires the most disciplines of a mixer," says Robert Scovill. "You have to deal with things on a sound system level, but you're also going to have to deal with things on a musical level, and that requires some insight and training into both those areas," he says. "You gotta know music to be able to talk to musicians, you gotta be able to know sound and physics to talk to system designers." Sound reinforcement engineers can be contracted for single events or tour for years; part of the excitement of this job is the opportunity to travel—but at the same time, you're living on catering and spending many long days, weeks, or months traveling with the same crew while you're missing your friends and family back home, and catching some of your favorite tour destinations through the window of your bus.

The front-of-house engineer is responsible for the mix the audience hears through the P.A. system; that's the person you see down in the crowd, working the console. The monitor mixer works alongside the stage, creating custom mixes for the musicians onstage, through earphones or "wedge" floor speakers, so that they can hear themselves perform. A system designer determines the type and configuration of gear to be used, including the P.A.

Remote engineers work on location at live events, recording and/or mixing them for broadcast feed, versus creating a mix for the audience. Remote recording environments can range from a portable rack of gear in a backstage room at a local concert to trucks outfitted with complete professional studios, at events such as the Grammys and the Academy Awards.

Theater sound involves placement of sound and effects design, as well as selecting and operating gear. And that's just the beginning, says Broadway theater sound designer Janet Kalas. "You have to know how to record people, you have to know how to set up a sound system, you have to know how to 'draft up' a system, you have to know how to talk to people," she says. "It's really an all-encompassing thing. It's not just setting up a system for one band every night, in a different theater. It's knowing how to deal with different theaters, and different shows, and different circumstances, and always, different people, setting up relationships all the time."

"Special venue" audio involves sound design and reinforcement for sports events, amusement parks, churches, and other locations. Jobs in this field include system and sound design, as well as live mixing. For example, theme park audio production encompasses everything from getting involved at the attraction-development stage to the creation of sound effects that will operate with animatronics and other special effects on high-tech thrill rides and attractions, to working on-site to manage the sound for live concerts and theatrical productions.

Film and Broadcast

There are three main audio elements of film: Dialog, sound effects, and music. Film sound is generally broken down into two phases, production and post-production. Production sound involves capturing source audio material, which varies from dialog on a set to sound effects in the field. Location recorders capture everything from actors speaking to birds chirping to howling wind gusts to "room noise."

There may be only a few people recording audio during production, but there are many more involved in post-production. Much of a film's dialog and effects are actually added later on in the studio during post-production, for clarity and accuracy. At this stage, ADR (Automatic Dialog Replacement) editors work with actors in the studio to re-record their lines to replace production dialog, which is edited by the dialog editor. Sound effects editors place effects in the movie, and Foley engineers work on a soundstage, manipulating various objects and materials in sync to picture, re-creating incidental sounds, such as footsteps, car-door slams, etc. A Foley walker creates the sounds, while a Foley mixer records them, and a Foley editor syncs them up with picture.

A music editor coordinates the film's music elements, including working with the composer to prepare to integrate the score with the other parts of the film, and choosing and placing songs and "source" music (heard in jukeboxes, radios, and other "onscreen" sources). Re-recording mixers then combine music, effects, and dialog, and the final mix is performed by a team that usually includes a dialog mixer, music mixer, and effects mixer.

Engineers who create audio for television perform many of these same functions, mixing or recording on location, or at an in-house studio, but the process is much faster. Something that might take a month in film would happen in only a week for TV. And the sound sources are simpler, often a single mic; also, they're often incorporating live sources. Because film and broadcast jobs are largely union, the roles are usually more clearly defined than those associated with music recording, but many of the skills required are the same.

Other Careers

Some of the fastest growing areas of audio production are in "new media" fields. There are tons of Web-production opportunities for those who have mastered HTML and multimedia authoring (programming and design) formats. Another booming field is the videogame industry, which is now even more lucrative than the film industry. Opportunities for audio engineers include working on staff at major game development houses, or doing contract sound effects, dialog, and music work. The exploding DVD market has also created a new demand for people who can author audio content, from wedding videographers to film producers.

Audio manufacturing jobs can be found in both hardware design and software programming. There are a variety of opportunities within those areas, from testing to product management, sales, and marketing.

Acousticians combine architecture with the science of sound; they design recording studios, concert halls, and other performance spaces, and design noise-control systems for restaurants, airports, and other public spaces. In general, most areas of design have an audio component, from city and highway planning to industrial design to aerospace engineering. Audio engineers even work in the automotive industry, noise-proofing car interiors and tuning engines.

With the growth of today's audio education programs, there are plenty of teaching opportunities, from panel moderator to tenured professor, depending on your qualifications and areas of interest. Have a flair for grammar? Writing opportunities range from reviewing products for trade magazines to writing product manuals for manufacturers, to publishing white papers and books.

Many large corporations and hotels have their own audio/video departments, to produce internal presentations and configure and maintain A/V systems. Audio engineers are even involved in crime solving, analyzing recordings for clues—a field known as forensic audio.

"It is a huge industry with many opportunities; most opportunities are not well known or publicized," says UMass Lowell's William Moylan. "I am continually amazed at the type of positions my students find. Two people who graduated from

UMass Lowell about ten years ago now have a very successful ring-tone company." If you keep an open mind and look beyond the studio environment, you'll find a wealth of opportunities, and one just may be perfect for you.

DO SOME CAREER DETECTIVE WORK

There's no better way to gain insight into a potential job than to get out there and talk to the people who are doing what you'd like to do. Arrange a field trip to a local facility, club, or TV or radio station. Track down some people who are working in a field you're interested in, and see if they're willing to give you a short informational interview. Quiz them about their work environment: The hours, types of projects, the pay, anything you'd like to know. Don't be afraid to ask a lot of questions! People are usually excited to talk about their work and are almost always willing to help a newbie. Ask about what a typical day is like. What are the best aspects of the job? And don't by shy about soliciting "negative" information: What do they like the least? What would they change, if they could? Sometimes a response that seems discouraging on the surface can be highly enlightening. For example, take the reasons one post-production engineer decided to leave the industry: "I've gotten tired of the pursuit," she says. "The problem with production is that it requires you to constantly pursue it, to constantly stay on top of it, to work much harder than it pays off. The pay is abysmal, the hours are long, and for every ten fantastic clients, there's one client who treats you like dirt. You have to put so much of yourself out there in a desperate attempt to garner the slightest reward, and frankly 99% of the time it's boring and mundane work. There's a lot of production work out there, but 90% has nothing to do with glamour or quality or even fun. I did session after session recording voice-overs for medical CDs and doing music placement in a toilet [paper] commercial—no joke—and working on internal corporate videos. I looked at what I was getting paid for that kind of work, then looked ahead to the guy who had the next-highest-paying position and thought about what he was doing day in and day out. Then I looked at the senior-most guy and looked at what he was doing day in and day out. Then I thought about how long it took him to get to the point where he could polish and deliver corporate videos and cell-phone spots, and I realized the effort was totally disproportionate to the payoff." She admits, however, that the job had its positive side: "On the other hand, my favorite part of the job was the freedom from being tied to a desk. I liked interacting with clients. I loved contributing to a project in a way that made a producer's eyes light up. I found satisfaction in the weirdest places, like coming in early and getting all of the suites arranged and ready for the day's sessions, and having the opportunity to say 'not a problem' to a client who was afraid his request would not be do-able."

There are a lot of other ways to research a field you're interested in. (These will be explored in depth in the Chapter Two: Your Game Plan.) The Internet is a great place to start: You'll find the most current information, and you may even end up making connections that could lead to informational interviews or other resources. Industry trade magazines regularly profile people in all of the careers mentioned above, and put much of their content online. Visit audio forums such as *prosoundweb.com, modernrecording.com,* or the newsgroup rec.audio.pro, to find out what people are saying about their jobs. Post a question or two, and see what kind of response you get. Check the library for industry books and trade magazines. There are many books out there about recording studios and the history of the recording industry. (*Temples of Sound* by Jim Cogan and William Clark is one of my favorites.) Some top engineers and producers have even written their own books; read them. Keep an eye out for local seminars and workshops. Industry associations such as the National Academy of Recording Arts and Sciences (NARAS, the association behind the Grammys), the Society of Professional Audio Recording Services (SPARS), and the Audio Engineering Society (AES) occasionally open their regional events and workshops to the public. Check their Websites for details. Schools and music stores also occasionally host free clinics and other events.

If you've done some career research, congratulations! You've already completed the first step in your job-hunting journey. Now that you're focused and you're confident that this is really, truly the job for you, you are ready to tackle the next step: Learning the skills you'll need.

Crystal Davis
AOL Music Editor

"I wanted to do something that was less internally cerebral, more interactive."

If it wasn't for a chance temp job assignment, Crystal Davis would probably not have a career in audio production. A few years ago, the UC Berkeley philosophy/psychology major was wrestling with the direction her educational path was taking, feeling dissatisfied with her academic community and at odds with the curriculum. "I didn't want to do something that was so idiosyncratic and relied on a really small field of experience—not just what you knew but what also you would be able to process through a career," she says. "I felt like my academic path was really limiting, when I really wanted to do something that was not really less cerebral, but less internally cerebral, more interactive."

A musician from the age of five, Davis had recently begun to play pretty seriously, and was considering transferring to a music school when she landed a short-term job at the Ex'pression College for Digital Arts (Emeryville, California). "It was totally by accident," she says. "I was temping while I was in school, part time, and I ended up being placed there for a few months." She had also spent the past couple of years DJ'ing and producing college radio, and had enjoyed picking up some basic recording and editing techniques there; being at Ex'pression suddenly catalyzed her interest. She enrolled in the program and instantly immersed herself in the curriculum. "At first I thought I'd be more interested in integrating recording with acoustic sources and recording my own self and capturing that sound," she says. "I was also interested in studio design at that point, too—in sound reflections. Every time you go through a different quarter, your interest changes, because you get so immersed. It's so much fun. You think, 'I could do this for a really long time.'"

Davis kept up her radio gig, while dabbling in Internet radio on a show she produced with one her teachers, Bill Turner, for Chuck D. Meanwhile, she spent as much time as possible recording various ensembles at school. "I was into a lot of acoustic, hip hop," she says. "Since I'm a DJ, I have a lot of access to musicians who need help with tracking and mix tapes. So I got a lot of practice recording small groups and large groups like jazz ensembles. I spent a lot of time trying to understand what kinds of techniques people were using on other albums, but at the same time I was also looking at sound design and post-production and trying to do a little bit of everything, and become really well rounded in my understanding of audio."

After Davis graduated, she interned in corporate A/V and ended up getting hired on to do some part-time work, but she says she didn't really enjoy the job. "I ended up leaving because I felt overworked and underappreciated, and I was getting called in at all sorts of odd hours. It was really getting fatiguing," she says. "I saw myself possibly working at a studio, but I didn't like the experiences that I was hearing about from friends who were interning in local studios. They were at great studios, but they just felt like they were slaves and not getting paid. I really didn't want something like that. I also wanted to do some sound design, but I felt like I didn't have enough practical experience doing that. I was trying to work a little bit on my own."

Meanwhile, Ex'pression had started a show with Sirius satellite radio called "Ex'pression Hours," and it needed a producer. "I took that, even though the pay was really bad," she says. "When you start out, you'll either get no pay or the pay's going to be really bad, so you want to make sure you like doing it." Davis ran with the opportunity, calling on both her radio experience and her impressive network of musicians. "I encouraged a lot of groups to come in and do live sets as much as possible. I did some jazz sets, did a lot of DJ sets," she says. "We focused on entertainment. I was able to use a lot of my contacts from just knowing musicians, having people on my radio show over the past years, and knowing a lot of promoters. I was able to have a lot of people like Grand Master Flash, Less McCann, Zap Mama, and had some actors like Danny Hoche [*Black Hawk Down*]."

The Sirius program led to a gig at America Online. Today, Davis works as an editor for AOL's Music Now 26 channel, spending about half her time at the company's corporate facility and half in her home studio, preparing audio files for the Web channel. "They send material in, and I clean it up, encode it, and make sure it's ready for our player. I do some ID production and some promo/commercial production for them myself. Sometimes I'll do content for a whole channel if it's a promotional channel, like one we did for the Superbowl, and I did almost everything for that, spotting music, editing them all together, making something smooth and continuous." When she's not editing for AOL, Davis divides the rest of her time among DJ'ing, playing music, and engineering band projects.

Reflecting back on her career path, Crystal Davis says she never knew she wanted to get into the audio industry, but is happy about the way her career turned out. "It was a surprising choice, but a good one."

CHAPTER TWO

YOUR GAME PLAN

The previous chapter gave you just a small dose of the type of skills you'll need and the range of jobs you might pursue. The next step, acquiring skills, will lay the foundation for a lifetime of learning. There are endless education routes, from learning on the job to investing years in advanced degrees, and no single path works for everyone. This chapter will define your options for entering the world of audio. It's up to you to research them carefully and come up with an action plan.

CREATIVE EXPRESSION THROUGH TECHNOLOGY

This industry is a marriage of art and science, and being successful requires a unique combination of technological aptitude and creativity. The talent, you are born with. But you learn skills. And how and what you learn will shape your career path. It's important to note here that it's not always the best technical engineer who gets the gig. There are many other factors at play: Some very successful engineers aren't technically "the best" at engineering, but they have studied their art and the business and know how to provide a higher level of service in general to their clients. The point? Being an engineer is a package deal. "Today's studio engineer has to know a number of tasks, such as how to put the studio online, some basic video-editing skills, obviously comprehensive Pro Tools skills," says Tom Misner, founder of the international School of Audio Engineering (SAE). "In other words, a studio engineer today must have many more skills but specialize in recording and mixing sound." There are many skills and talents you must bring to the table. Identify your weaknesses and try to overcome them. If you can't, compensate by excelling in another area. Being balanced makes you more marketable.

"There's two different approaches [to recording], and to be successful you have to kind of hit it in the middle," says legendary recording engineer Bruce Swedien. "One way is to approach what we do from the purely technical side. The other way is to approach it from the musical side. Neither one will get you all the way. It has to be a combination." So, the recording process is an unusual paradox: You must be fluent in technological tools as a necessary part of a creative production process. But to be successful, you need to look at these technical tools as just that: A means to get your job done. The tools alone aren't going to do it. You need to understand how to select, combine, and use them to achieve the results you want—just like a construction worker uses many tools together to build the house; or a painter employs a palette of colors to create a work of art. This is all part of the learning process.

THE IMPORTANCE OF EDUCATION

"Not every student will make a great assistant engineer, and not every great assistant will have the set of skills it takes to become a great recording engineer," says AES president Theresa Leonard, who also serves as director of audio, music, and sound at the Banff Centre. "Those with a unique gift will stand out above the rest, regardless of what program or training they might have. However, the proper training and mentoring—as well as the right connections—can help direct these individuals on a path that will lead to a successful career."

The audio industry itself is relatively young, and as recently as a few decades ago, formal audio educational programs didn't exist. Many people who have been in this business for fifteen, twenty years, or more found success by working their way up on the job. But these days, it's virtually impossible to walk into a production facility without any skills and expect them to take you under their wing. Even if you volunteer, they might not be paying you, but you're taking up time and space, and studios today rarely have the luxury to train potential employees on the basics. They just don't have the resources. "The studio or audio facility demands that you have a certain amount of entry-level knowledge to become a useful member of a studio team, and they are not willing to train you because why should they pay for your training when you can pay for it yourself? Studios and audio facilities prefer you to know 'enough,' so they can teach you 'more,'" says School of Audio Engineering's Tom Misner.

"I don't think anyone hires an entry-level employee with the idea they will immediately handle their best clients," says Larry Lipman, former SPARS director and audio educational consultant. "Instead, they are looking for someone with potential—to season in their facility—but they expect that person to arrive with solid fundamentals."

Full Sail's Nell Thompson says employers contacting her school looking for rookies seek candidates with three specific attributes: "Those that have the drive, passion, and commitment to this industry and the clients they serve; a willingness to start at the bottom and stay there as long as it takes; and the potential to step in and provide assistance when there is a need," she says. "In this age of deadlines and bottom lines, it is this third attribute that can separate those with training and those without. Who is ready to step up and provide technical assistance under pressure when needed?"

"The need for employees, even beginning-level employees, to thoroughly understand and be able to utilize computer skills and other advanced technologies has made it necessary for companies to acknowledge the need for some type of education in their hiring," adds UMass Lowell's William Moylan. "I've noticed, now that recording programs have been around for twenty years, that people doing the hiring that have a formal education in recording value education highly, and will seek to hire someone with an education.

"There are still industry people around who learned how to clean a toilet before they learned how to clean a tape head," he says. "While they can still be prone to wanting to see hires 'pay their dues,' perhaps even before being entered on the payroll, most of the 'old school' industry people have come to value formal education of one type or another. Hires without some type of preparation are becoming more and more rare. I would say you can still get into the industry by learning the ropes on the job—if all the stars align correctly on the special day you cross the path of one of the few people willing to take a shot on someone with little or no training—but chances are much poorer than they once were."

There are a million different motivations for hiring people, especially in a creative industry. I've heard it all: A studio manager once told me he liked to hire people who went to "better" (read: expensive) schools, because it showed "financial commitment" to their career. One New York engineer told me he got hired simply because he was wearing a cowboy shirt and the studio manager loved country music! Thankfully, these days what you know is a lot more important, but the stakes get higher all the time. Chances are, nobody's going to want to see your diploma during a job interview. But they *do* expect you to demonstrate that you've learned the skills, and this is where your education is key.

A good education teaches you how to *assimilate* information and make use of what you learn. Think of school as the framework, the context in which you'll place your work experience. In other words, you'll learn a lot in the studio, but what you learn will make a lot more sense if you have a good grasp of the fundamentals. Likewise, you'll never move on to engineer status if you don't grasp the fundamentals of being an assistant. You may not have all the answers, but you'll know where to find them and having that confidence will enable you to turn challenges into opportunities. School offers built-in support infrastructure, whether you're learning mixing tips or job hunting. Another benefit of formalized training is that it teaches you general methodology that you can apply to any situation, as opposed to learning specific (and possibly even outdated or incorrect) methods on the job. ("This is how *we* do it at *this* company.") The physics of sound will never change, no matter where you end up in the industry. In other words, the fundamentals of audio are the same, but the application will always be different. And although technologies often change faster than our ability to master them, it's important to have a knowledge base that you can apply to new technologies and new situations.

It's easy to teach technology, explains Larry Lipman, "There's a piece of gear out there, and it's very easy to say it does a, b, c, and d, and this is how it works, and this is the science behind it, and these are the settings, and when you make this adjustment, this is technically what happens. To then take technical knowledge and teach someone how to use that information artistically, and do so with personality in a recording session where you are helping to create magic, not detract from it, that's the difficult part."

"For example, I strive not to teach a specific recording console, but rather to teach the concepts of consoles," Lipman continues. "I'll give you an example from my past. Now understand, I didn't do this to make a point, it just happened this way. I'm visually impaired. We were in the midst of a major renovation of the recording studio at The University of Memphis. I had to teach my students some console fundamentals, and because our facility was shut down due to the renovation, I had made some arrangements to borrow time in studios around town. It just so happens that I had never been to this particular studio before, and they had a new console that I had never seen before. I sat in the back of the control room, placed my students up at the console, and said, 'Okay, look for something called a mic trim or mic pre,' and I just went down through the whole system with them. We got sound through the console without a problem. I wasn't trying to show off or make a point, I just knew that with my vision trouble I wasn't going to be able to hover over the console and find what I needed; it was better for them to do the work anyway. At the end they turned to me and said, 'Now we see why learning the concepts is important, because you keep telling us this and we keep blowing you off, but we know you've never seen this equipment and yet you're sitting in the back of the control room leading us through using this console.'"

There are a lot of people with technical skills, but fewer who can really analyze and process information; those who don't just know solutions, but know *how* to look for a solution, will have a career edge. Consider this "tale of two interns" from *Mix* magazine editorial director George Petersen: "If I had a facility right now and I was going to hire two people, and they both knew how to push the buttons on an SSL console or how to work Pro Tools, and one of the people knew a little bit about electronics and could fix a microphone cable—or at least tell me if the microphone cable was broken—that's the person who's going to get the nod." As an example, he describes a scenario in which two interns get jobs in different recording studios, and they both go to work and they have to record vocals for a voice-over session, but the main engineer is sick. In each case, they are confident that they know the gear and volunteer for the session. "They both plug in the microphone, set it up, turn on the console, and pull up the fader, and guess what? No sound," he says. "Now, one of these people is going to run around in circles and start switching cables at random, and pulling the microphone out, and the other person, who's a little bit more savvy about signal flow and troubleshooting, will look at it and think okay, logically, maybe there's something in the console. The easiest thing to do is switch inputs and see if it works. And maybe if that person did that right away, he would find out that one of the modules in the console is bad, or maybe it was something as simple as the phantom power switch on the console was out. So, the person who understands signal flow and troubleshooting a little bit will fix the problem in thirty seconds and the session will continue. With the other person, after fifteen minutes of running around in circles and changing mic cables and changing windscreens and not knowing what the heck to do, pretty soon the client will just get up and walk out and never come back to that studio. The employee can say, 'Well, the equipment was faulty.' Well, yeah, it might be faulty, but it happens a lot, and you have to think fast. Time is money, and people want things done."

RESEARCH THE JOB BEFORE COMMITTING TO SCHOOL

First things first: You're curious about this career, right? Well, get out there and do some detective work. (Hopefully, by now you've started this research process as part of the plan described in Chapter One, Assistant Engineering 101.) Call your local studio or TV station and find out if you can arrange an educational visit. It's great idea to visit someone who's doing what you want to do, just to get an idea of what the day-to-day job is really like. If you've already done this, let's take this to the next level: If you are interested, consider volunteering; even just observing out in the field before you start classes will really enhance your book learning. Ask around; you never know who knows someone who's doing what you're interested in. This industry is all about networking, and savvy networking is an art that must be developed. You might as well start practicing now.

If you're still in high school, ask your guidance counselor or music teacher for help. Perhaps he or she has some contacts in the community and could arrange for a field trip to a recording studio. Don't panic if your counselor tries to persuade you to become a lawyer instead of a recording engineer. Some people don't understand why someone would want a fulfilling career in an industry they love instead of making a boatload of money. Ask for help at school, but if no one is willing to help, forget them and head out on your own. If you really want this career, you will find a way to follow your heart.

Top live sound engineer and professor Robert Scovill advises potential students to first go out and get their feet wet. "It doesn't matter at what level, if you can get into some clubs, high schools, churches, I don't care. Just start doing something," he says, adding that it's ideal to get some exposure *before* your classroom training. "What we do is such an abstract thing. You can't see sound. Just by getting exposed to the technology a little bit, when you then take some formal training on it, your retention will be so much better. Because if you just walk into the school, you get bomb-blasted with the abstractness of it. Until you hear it and turn some knobs and experience something, it's hard to put your finger on it."

Other ideas: Scour the Internet. There are a lot of highly opinionated audio forums, chatrooms, and newsgroups out there (*rec.audio.pro* and *prosoundweb.com* are good places to start). Anonymity can foster brutal career honesty online. It wouldn't hurt to lurk around in some forums that interest you, and even post some questions to find out what kinds of skills and education people are looking for in the field you're researching. Ask them what they look for in potential employees. Ask them about themselves: Did they go to school? How well did their education prepare them? You might even convince people to tell you how much money they make. Be street-smart, though. Make sure you don't confuse personal views with facts! Although it's valuable to gain insight from those who have "been there, done that," take opinions with a grain of salt!

Still not sure if this is the right career move for you? Before you make the commitment to quit your day job or change your major midstream, you might want to try it on for size by enrolling in some local night courses or take a weekend seminar or two, to see if you even enjoy mixing. I've even heard of people taking the unusual, if admittedly luxurious, route of booking studio time just to watch and learn how it all works, by videotaping their session with a willing engineer.

What Type of Program is Best?

Most veteran engineers tell me that, back in the day, they had to learn the ropes on the job; those who did go to school say they chose their educational path by default, because they "didn't know any better," or "didn't have any options." Today, there's no excuse for not finding a curriculum that's perfectly tailored to your goals; there are plenty of focused, quality programs. Hundreds of options are available, from Web courses to two-week hands-on seminars to postgraduate degrees; and you can choose from music-based, business-based, engineering-based, or interdisciplinary programs.

School is a major commitment, however. To some, that commitment might mean putting in a few months of intensive hands-on learning. To others, it may mean investing many years of full-time study (and tens of thousands of dollars) toward advanced degrees. The amount of time and money you want to dedicate is entirely up to you, and only you can decide which path is best for your needs. Take a hard look at yourself and your goals, interests, and abilities. This is a multidisciplinary career, and there are a number of educational routes to take. For detailed information about the major educational programs, see the Resources section in the back of this book. For our purposes at this point, what follows is a general description of the types of programs you may want to pursue.

Music-Based

Maybe music is your true love. Dozens of colleges and universities, such as UMass

Lowell, Ithaca College, UMiami, and New York University have large music schools that offer major and minor degree programs in recording. Many of these programs combine traditional music studies and math, engineering, and physics coursework with an audio track that includes both theoretical work and hands-on production. Some schools, such as Johns Hopkins University's Peabody Institute, the University of Hartford's Hartt School of Music, and Oberlin Conservatory's TIMARA (Technology In Music And Related Arts) department combine a conservatory environment with audio studies. Berklee College of Music offers a four-year Bachelor's degree or four-year professional diplomas, including a program in music synthesis and music production and programming. Generally, to be admitted to a university-level music-based program, you'll have to pass an initial audition as a vocalist or instrumentalist, in addition to meeting the program's academic requirements.

Industry/Business Specialty

Perhaps you're considering a business-based degree. There are many advantages to going this route: If your goal is to run your own audio company someday, you'll get the foundation you need to market your services and build a successful operation. Having business savvy gives you a leg up on engineers who may not be able to contribute beyond their audio skills. And, if you ever decide to leave the industry, you'll have the universal skills that make you employable in any field.

Many schools combine sound recording programs with business or communications: Belmont University in Nashville offers a Bachelor's of business administration with emphasis in music production. Middle Tennessee State University offers a B.S. in production and technology through its Recording Industry department in its college of mass communication.

Engineering Focus

Maybe you find the idea of building a circuit board a lot more intriguing than miking a drum. If you're interested in equipment design and troubleshooting, consider a program with an electrical engineering or computer science focus, or perhaps combine your major with a minor in electrical engineering. With interdisciplinary-programs that have been around for more than 25 years, UMiami offers a Music Engineering technology program that includes a minor in electrical engineering or computer science. UMiami also offers a Bachelor of Science in Electrical Engineering with an emphasis in audio engineering. Case Western Reserve University in Cleveland offers a four-year B.A. in audio recording or a five-year double major with electrical engineering.

Program Lengths

Audio programs range in length and scope from one-day seminars to post-graduate research. Whether you have a weekend, a summer, or a few years to spare, you can find a program to fit your needs.

Seminars, Short Courses, Web Programs

Still in high school? The Fred N. Thomas Career Education Center offers an audio program for junior and senior high-school students in the Denver metro area. More and more vocational schools, such as Ocean County Vocational Technical Schools in Lakehurst, New Jersey, are designing audio certificate programs for high school and post-secondary students, so check near you.

Web courses provide an ideal learning environment if you're unable to travel to a school or find it difficult fitting classwork into a hectic job schedule. *Berkleemusic.com,* the Web branch of the Berklee College of Music, offers a variety of online music-production classes, ranging from six to twelve weeks in length. Students receive and post assignments, and collaborate with other students and instructors, entirely over the Internet.

Short courses and seminars can give you an introduction to a topic, fill gaps in your education, or just enhance your career skills in general. Perhaps you're interested in a specialized topic. Got a day or two? Catch a local stop on a touring seminar series from outfits such as Fits and Starts Productions (*www. modernrecording.com*) or Synergetic Audio Concepts (*www.synaudcon.com*). The New York Institute for Forensic Audio in Colonia, New Jersey, holds training classes every year in forensic voice identification. You can also hone your skills on a specific system: Pro Tools certification can be found in any region of the country, from Future Media Concepts in New York City to The Pro Tools Training Center in Miami to the Mindlab Learning Centers in the San Francisco Bay area. You can even take courses in real, working audio facilities, such as those offered by Ardent Studios in Memphis; Omega Recording Studios in Rockville, Maryland; Sheffield Audio/Video Productions in Phoenix, Maryland; or Parsons Audio, a Boston pro-audio dealer.

The opportunities are endless. How about combining learning with a spectacular mountain setting? Try the Aspen Music Festival's Edgar Stanton Recording Institute four-week seminar, or perhaps the Banff Centre in the Canadian Rockies, where you can enroll in audio workshops, residencies, and programs developed in conjunction with Stanford University's CCRMA (Center for Computer Research in Music and Acoustics) program, a multidisciplinary facility where composers and researchers work together using computer-based technology for both art and research.

Certificate/One-Year/Two-Year Programs

Short-term audio production programs can provide immediate hands-on experience, allowing you to gain skills to enter the job market sooner, or perhaps to supplement a two- or four-year degree in a "peripheral" discipline, such as electrical engineering or computer programming. If you're looking for an immersive audio experience, you've got a lot of choices, with programs ranging from a few weeks to a few years. The Recording Workshop in Chillicothe, Ohio, offers a five-week,

180-hour program in recording engineering and music production, with one-week optional add-ons in maintenance and troubleshooting, and other advanced topics. The SAE Institute of Technology (locations worldwide) offers nine-month full-time, and 18-month part-time diploma programs in audio and multimedia, and the Los Angeles Recording Workshop's 900-hour recording engineer certificate program takes about thirty weeks to complete. The Conservatory of Recording Arts & Sciences near Phoenix offers a 37-week full-time certificate program.

While some hands-on trade schools provide a certificate or diploma, and others such as the Institute of Audio Research in New York City and some SAE schools offer degree credit at participating colleges and universities, some audio schools offer degrees of their own.

Full Sail Real World Education in Winter Park, Florida, for example, used to offer diplomas but has developed into Associate and Bachelor degree programs. The Ex'pression College for Digital Arts near San Francisco grants Associate and Bachelor degrees on an accelerated schedule. (The Bachelor in Sound Arts is a two-and-a-half year program.)

If you're looking for more of a liberal arts program, some schools offer Associate degrees or similar certificates as part of their general curriculum. Guilford Technical Community College in Jamestown, North Carolina, offers an Associate degree in both sound engineering and concert sound and lighting, and New England School of Communications in Bangor, Maine, has a two-year Associate of Science in Communications program with an audio engineering concentration. UCLA Extension offers certificate programs in recording engineering and film scoring, and the Vancouver Film School has a one-year diploma in sound design.

University Programs

University programs, whether they emphasize music or engineering, combine advanced audio theoretical and practical studies with liberal arts. I've mentioned a few programs above, but there are hundreds more to choose from, each with a unique curriculum and focus. Audio programs have evolved to the point where you can find a specific program to meet your academic needs, whether you plan to specialize in film scoring, sound reinforcement, or acoustics. For example, the Yale School of Drama, the University of Cincinnati Conservatory of Music, and the University of Missouri, Kansas City all offer graduate degrees in theater sound design. San Francisco State University offers a B.A. or M.A. in Radio and TV with emphasis in music recording, and Columbia College in Chicago offers Bachelor degrees in a variety of audio fields, including concert sound reinforcement, sound contracting, and sound for picture. Northeastern University in Boston offers a B.S. in music technology with an emphasis in composition for new media.

It used to be that a graduate program in audio was unheard of. Today there are dozens of schools offering advanced degrees, so how far you want to take your education is entirely up to you. NYU offers a two-year Masters in Music in music technology, focusing on scoring for film and multimedia, or a Tonmeister honors sequence; McGill University in Montreal offers an M.M. in sound recording; and Penn State and Johns Hopkins offer Masters programs that focus on acoustics. Minnesota State University in Moorhead grants M.M.s in new media, and the University of Colorado Denver has an M.A. program with an emphasis in technology or audio forensics.

Do You Need A Degree?

The decision to pursue a college degree is a big one. Should you go for it? It depends on what you hope to gain from your formal education. There's no question that a college degree provides a well-rounded education, exposing you to so much more than audio, through both required coursework and electives that you choose, including humanities, ethics, languages, and science. You may think that some of that "peripheral" coursework won't ever relate to your mixing job, but it all contributes to your well-roundedness as a person. You'll learn strong analytical skills, which apply to any discipline. And, it's something you can always fall back on if you ever decide to work in a different field (or if you need to pick up extra work in lean times). The university environment also exposes you to a diverse community; you'll be exposed to people from a variety of backgrounds, on a variety of career paths. The trade-offs? With a few exceptions, universities are much more expensive than trade schools, and you'll need to dedicate a longer period of time to your education.

Academy Award-winning production sound mixer Arthur Rochester says his time in college, albeit medical school, gave him a basic foundation for learning that transcended professions. "Never discount the value of a good formal education," he says. "A college education teaches so much more than how to do a job. It teaches basic problem-solving skills that are necessary in daily life. It teaches how to ask the right questions. It teaches how to find all the information needed to answer the questions that must be answered. A college education gives the skills necessary to choose a leader to follow, as well as to lead a following. It imparts a set of values that allow us to make proper decisions. Most importantly, a formal college education imparts a discipline that is the foundation for all learning. I recommend, at least, a formal education in the Liberal Arts. Four years, or more, spent learning the sciences is even better. I have no regrets about the years I spent in college."

Not everyone agrees that a degree is necessary. In most industries, some kind of formal training is required. (Would you go to a dentist who "learned on the job"?) But in this business that places so much importance on experience, some people believe that the clout a college degree brings is not as relevant here as in other industries that recognize a more traditional academic model. It may be more important to find a practical program (which may last any amount of time, from a few weeks to a year or two) that immerses students into all audio production, all the time, right away, from day one to the end, without dedicating time to "superfluous" academic endeavors. Top-quality, well-respected programs exist in both the trade school and university realms. No choice is right for everyone; your decision depends on how much time and money you can invest in school, and what you want to gain from it.

Regardless of how you feel about earning a degree, don't equate a program's length with its level of difficulty. America Online music editor Crystal Davis, who says she comes from a rigorous educational background, transferred midstream from a philosophy program at the University of California at Berkeley campus to the audio curriculum at nearby Ex'pression College for Digital Arts and found that, although the academic focus was completely different, the short-term immersion program was just as demanding as her university experience. "Going through the [Ex'pression] program was really difficult, but it is for everybody; no-one has an easy time there," she says. "It's definitely not something that people should take lightly. There were people there who felt like this would be easier than a four-year college, but it definitely wasn't."

Most importantly, no matter which path you choose, it's tempting to seek out the quickest and easiest path to learning. But in doing so, you can do yourself a disservice. Don't make shortcuts when it comes to your education; this is your career we're talking about. You're in this for the long haul. Keep your perspective long-term: Remember, in this high-tech field, you're pretty much guaranteed that, with the lightning-speed evolution of technology, ten years down the road this industry will look nothing like what you see right now, and you want to lay a foundation now that will enable you to adapt to changes throughout your career. Learning is not instant gratification; you want your education to prepare you not just for your first job, but your second job, and your tenth job.

Berklee professor Stephen Webber says the most important lessons he teaches are critical thinking, problem solving, and the value of lifelong learning. "When I teach my students which button to push, their education has a six-month expiration date," he says. "If I lead them to discover why they need to push the button, and how to figure out any system they will run into in the future, then their education has a lifetime guarantee."

SELECTING A SCHOOL

Once you've decided which type of program is right for you, you'll need to evaluate the schools. This will feel like a daunting task at first, but one that will get easier as you progress. You'll begin to streamline the process and narrow your choices with each school you research.

Begin the search process early; many schools have admission deadlines, and you don't want to rush your decision. A school directory is a great point of departure for your research. There's a short list in the back of this book to help you get started. You can find school guides in any bookstore, but a directory of audio programs will be a lot more useful. *Mix* magazine publishes an annually updated directory; you can find it at *www.mixonline.com*. The Audio Engineering Society also publishes a directory on its Website, *www.aes.org*. No single program is right for everyone, so make sure you've outlined your needs clearly before you begin your search.

Research carefully. The more you investigate, the more you'll notice reputations emerge. Request catalogs and brochures, and visit the campus whenever possible. Remember that schools (even universities) are businesses, and the information you receive is designed to draw you in as a "customer." The more reputable the school, the more the curriculum and facilities will speak for themselves, and the less it relies on marketing to "sell" itself. Be aware that you can't always judge a school by glossy brochures or slick Websites. You have to be savvy and filter through the promotional pitch to find the real nuts and bolts of the program.

It's really difficult to determine a school's true "success rate," but most schools make it a point to showcase graduates who are working in the field. Actual verifiable lists of employed grads will tell you a lot more about the placement success of the program than general statistics like, "We place more than 100 graduates in the industry annually," when "in the industry" might mean Tower Records. Also, make sure they can show you grads working in advanced careers, not just in entry-level positions.

Talk to the faculty, talk to the students. You'll probably get the most honest feedback about a program from recent graduates, so ask the school for some names. Contact them. Ask them what they liked most—and least—about the program. Did they like the teachers? Was there a good balance of theory and hands-on? Did they get enough studio time? Were they given a realistic perspective of the industry? Were the studios and gear dedicated to student use only, or was the school booking them out for paid sessions too? Did they get help finding work after graduation? Was the gear current? If they were starting over, would they choose the same program again?

Considerations

Take a hard look at the curriculum: Make sure there's plenty of hands-on work to balance theory classes. (Reading about audio is sort of like talking about driving a car: Until you get behind the wheel, you're only halfway there. All the theory in the world isn't going to prepare you for driving on the freeway at rush hour.) Determine when you'll actually be able to get into a studio; will you be able to dig in relatively early in the program, or is studio time reserved until later? (Don't expect a school to set you loose in their studios right away without knowing you can handle the technology, but watch out if overall studio time seems inordinately limited. It could be a sign that there are inadequate facilities to handle student traffic, or just that the program is to skewed toward book learning.)

Are you learning about different aspects of recording, such as live sound, post-production, and multimedia? How about MIDI sequencing, video production, and acoustics? Some programs also include a class or two on business, which is useful.

Equipment maintenance skills are important. Ideally, you should learn to troubleshoot gear, wire patchbays, and repair cables and headphones. The best maintenance courses will even teach you how to build simple gear circuits, applying your knowledge of electronics and hands-on skills like soldering. In an age when fewer and fewer studios keep maintenance engineers on staff, your fix-it chops could edge you past the competition in the job hunt.

Find out if the school teaches "old school" analog technology, such as tape-machine alignment. Yes, we're in the digital age, but it's still essential to understand the "old school" basics, because they are the foundation upon which new technology is developed. "I've probably spent as much time in my Pro Tools classes talking about where things came from," says Miami-based engineer and Pro Tools instructor Mihai Boloni. "For instance, in the tape days, we had a certain set of responsibilities—aligning tape machines, biasing tape, doing track sheets, doing session sheets, setting up the studio for a new session, recalling parameters—and now with computers, we're seeing a lot of people getting really lazy. They think that the computer's going to handle everything for them. We've taken one set of responsibilities and morphed them to another set. It's just as important now to name your tracks in Pro Tools, for instance, as it was to write them down on the track sheet and write it down on the board tape, where it was coming back in. A lot of people seem to overlook this."

If the program is interdisciplinary, determine if the focus is aligned with your educational goals. Do you want to learn electronics circuit theory? Web design? Scoring? Video production? Scout out coursework tailored to your needs.

How long ago was the program established? Of course, take this information in context of other variables such as facilities, teacher résumés, etc. A program's age isn't necessarily a gauge of quality, but it can be an indicator of experience. Don't assume that a program is better just because it has been around a long time. (In fact, the opposite can even be true, if the curriculum hasn't adapted with the times.) But if the school just opened last semester, there's a good chance there are still some kinks that need to be worked out.

Although there is no specific accreditation body for audio programs, organizations such as the National Association of Schools of Music (NASM), the Accrediting Commission of Career Schools and Colleges of Technology (ACCSCT), the National Association of Trade and Technical Schools (NATTS), or state and federal departments of education offer more general accreditation. This pedigree does not guarantee a great audio education, but you can be reasonably confident that the school is reputable. (And, conversely, a lack of accreditation doesn't necessarily categorize a program as inferior. Treat each situation on a case-by-case basis.)

"As Education Chair of the AES, I have been asked to come up with standard curriculums for audio education. This is extremely difficult to do," says Theresa

Leonard. "Although audio education programs are viewed in a higher light within the industry today, because of good programs that have been around for some time, these programs are varied. Some exist within music programs, some are aligned with a science degree, others stand on their own. What is most important in this industry is mentoring. The success of any program will depend on the instructors, not the curriculum." Examine instructor credentials: Do they have enough industry experience to share a broad range of skills? Is their experience current? You don't want some kid who just graduated last spring guiding you along your career path. But on the other hand, it's important to learn about technology from someone whose most recent recording session doesn't predate the compact disc.

What kind of facilities does the school offer? The campus should include enough audio recording studios to handle student volume, plus MIDI, video, and audio workstation-based editing suites, and a variety of recording spaces, including tracking rooms and live performance halls. What kind of equipment does the school work on? Check out gear lists. Although there's no way for any educational institution to keep up with each new technology as it debuts, some schools are better-funded than others, or they have close working relationships with equipment manufacturers, both of which can mean access to newer technologies and current gear. It's important to learn on equipment that closely parallels what you might find in a modern facility. But don't equate the "cool factor" with quality of education. There's certainly something to be said for mastering the intricacies of a state-of-the-art SSL console, but what happens when you show up at work and the console is a Neve? Your skills need to transcend an equipment feature set. You need to learn *why* things work the way the do, not just *how* they work.

The school should provide plenty of career counseling and job placement resources. Ideally, it should also hold career events such as résumé prep workshops. Most reputable schools require internships as part of their programs, and many offer credit for work-study. What kind of internship placement assistance does the school offer? Does it have placement relationships with reputable facilities? And for that matter, is its network limited to the local community, or is it plugged in nationwide? Are students left to seek out internships on their own? What other kinds of career services does the school offer?

You're probably seriously concerned about financial obligation, especially because not only will you spend a lot of money on school now but you won't be raking in the cash right out of the gate. What options are available at your potential school for loans, grants, scholarships, or aid? There are also many alternatives for attaining scholarships and other aid on your own. In addition to federal Pell Grants, work study programs, and loans (see *www.ed.gov* for information), there are millions of dollars available from private organizations, for regional scholarships, scholarships by major, minority groups, international students, the list goes on. Use your local library or the Web to learn about your options. There are even scholarships offered exclusively for audio students, such as the Mix Foundation's

TEC Awards education scholarship and the Motion Picture Sound Editors' Ethel Crutcher scholarship fund, part of the Verna Fields Award for Sound Editing in a Student Film, plus grant programs from the Society of Professional Audio Recording Services (SPARS) and the AES.

Skywalker Sound's Leslie Ann Jones, who plays a large role in selecting new hires for the scoring stage, says that the best educational programs are those that offer the most diversity in terms of options. "I would not look to a school that is only going to teach you how to be a recording engineer," she says. "I would look to a school that is going to teach you how to record sound for video games, and how to mix live sound, and how to master, and how to get yourself out of trouble with Pro Tools. Because when you get to the outside, you don't know what kind of jobs are going to be available, number one. And number two, you can find yourself in a job and all of a sudden an opportunity presents itself, and if you've had at least some training and nobody has to hand you a glossary with the job that explains in detail what every bit is, you're much more prepared to jump into one of those jobs." It's up to you to determine whether a program is qualified to fit your needs, so make an informed decision.

MAKING THE MOST OF YOUR EDUCATION

Once you're in school, make every minute count to maximize your experience there. Your learning shouldn't end in the classroom. Take this opportunity to get involved in extracurricular activities. You'll boost your practical knowledge and you'll start cultivating your own professional network.

At School, Outside the Classroom

Larry Lipman stresses that students begin earning their professional reputations the day they set foot on campus. "Your peer group is going to be looking at you, your professors are going to be looking at you, and while that's a lot to put on a young adult, especially when I think your time at college should be a lot of fun, I also think that you just have to remember that you are establishing an image for yourself," he says. "You have to present yourself professionally and deliver more than you promise. You need to show that you're easy to get along with; you're very dependable. You need to get active and involved in your industry from day one."

Stephen Webber stresses the importance of networking early, with your own peers as well as with the pros, "not just meeting people who are already successful, but people who are at about the same place in their careers as you are, who you identify as having the potential to become successful," he says. "I often joke that the most valuable thing my students get out of coming to Berklee is a network of college buddies." Don't limit your circle to the audio students. Get out and mingle with other academic departments. Talk to film students, graphic design majors, computer programmers.

In this industry, who you know can make all the difference in job hunting, and the sooner you begin building your network, the better. Here's a smart business investment: For about the cost of a case of beer, you can print up a professional set of business cards. (Some Web companies such as *Vistaprint.com* will even print you a set for free.) It's a good idea to carry them with you all the time, especially at events where you'll be meeting people with whom you'll want to remain in touch.

Consider your career network to be a support system. It's important to find mentors and role models early on, and to build a community that will assist you along the way throughout your career. "Mentoring is an important part of networking," says MTSU's Chris Haseleu. "Having someone in the industry that really knows your skills and your ambitions can be very helpful in finding that first gig. Later on, being a mentor is a great way to give a little back to the industry and to your school."

Mentors can be anyone you find inspiring or has helped guide you on your path, whether they're professionals in the field, teachers, friends, your boss, or even family members. "My father was a role model to me, and he was in the restaurant business," says studio designer Chris Pelonis. "He was a mentor as far as the work ethic was concerned and the 'never give up, nothing's impossible' kind of attitude."

No education comes with a guarantee of job placement. This sounds cliché, but it's true: What you get out of school is directly proportional to what you put in. Make the most out of your education. You need to be proactive, both inside and outside the classroom. There are a million ways to build experience: Offer to help teachers and other students with their projects. Volunteer at campus concert halls, performance spaces, and recording facilities. Some schools even allow students to assist in studio scheduling and maintenance and, sometimes, basic gear repair. The idea is to get your hands on as much gear as you can. Become as familiar with as many microphones as possible. Every mic imparts a unique "sound," which will become more and more apparent the more you use them. Learn the ins and outs of all of your school's outboard gear (equipment that is separate from the console). Become fluent in consoles and workstations. The more time you spend working out the kinks now, the more smoothly your sessions will run later.

Another great way to enhance your education while networking at the same time is to get involved in professional audio organizations. You'll make valuable contacts while developing your skills. Many professional organizations offer student memberships and may meet on your campus. The National Academy of Recording Arts and Sciences (NARAS), the organization behind the Grammy Awards, extends memberships to eligible students, who can even submit their recordings into the Grammy selection process. "There would be great benefits to a student joining NARAS," says Producers and Engineers wing director Leslie Lewis. "Just the fact that they would have the ability to enter their own recordings—if they happen to release something commercially—into the Grammy process, would be a tremendous thing for them, as well as being able to see the results of all these great veterans—great guidelines and recommendations for the future of music. It gives them access to a dialog that they might not otherwise have."

The Audio Engineering Society has chapters at many affiliated schools. Joining the AES gives you access to resources such as seminars held by visiting professionals, discounted admittance at conventions and other events, and subscription to a monthly scientific journal. Many AES student chapters arrange guest speakers, seminars, and workshops at their schools. Consider signing up or even running for office. Other organizations such as SPARS and the National Association of Record Industry Professionals hold regional seminars, workshops, and networking events. Check these out. They're a great way to learn about your craft while meeting professionals in the field and even pick up some career advice. Many associations hold annual or semi-annual conventions, and usually offer highly discounted student passes. Each show offers a different specialty, from NAB's (National Association of Broadcasters) TV and radio focus to South by Southwest's band showcases, but they are all great opportunities for both learning and networking. In addition to checking out the latest in products and technology demonstrations, you can sit in on educational panels, seminars, and workshops, often hosted by top producers and engineers. (See the Resources section in the back of the book to learn more about industry associations and events.)

Read the trade magazines! There are dozens of publications out there that are packed with practical how-to articles, reviews of the latest technology, interviews, and studio news. Here's where you'll get the most up-to-date information from top professionals in the field: You'll learn things like how Metallica is mixed on tour, where they got the ideas for the sound effects in *The Matrix*, and even what kind of gear they used to get that weird vocal effect on Cher. And not only will you learn about technology, the more you read these magazines, the better feeling you'll have for the business—who the movers and shakers are in the industry. Magazines such as *Mix, Electronic Musician, Remix, EQ,* and *Tape Op* feature the latest in new technology, tools, and applications, along with artist interviews, producer profiles, facility spotlights, album profiles, and studio news, while *Billboard, Variety, The Hollywood Reporter,* and *Pro Sound News* are slanted more toward newsy entertainment-biz content. Other magazines of interest will keep you on top of related industries: *Sound and Video Contractor* covers the A/V installation and special venue market, *Millimeter* is a film trade, *Post* and *Video Systems* magazines cover post-production, *Technologies for Worship* is pretty self-explanatory. *Live Sound* and *Pro Light and Staging News* report on the touring industry, and computer mags like *PC Week* and *MacWorld* keep you on top of key computer developments and applications to help you troubleshoot and streamline your workflow. Even today's top engineers say that reading these publications is crucial for them to keep abreast of the market as well as the latest in gear developments. If you're in school now, check and see if your campus receives free copies (and if they don't, ask if they can get them). If you can't subscribe to the magazines, maybe your local library carries them. At the very least, scour their Websites, which often feature daily news in addition to some or all of the current issue content, and article archives. (See the Resources section for more information about trade magazines.)

Beyond the Campus: Out in the Field

As your career aspirations evolve, now might be a good time to set up some informational interviews. These can be casual phone conversations, e-mailed questions, or personal visits—but the idea is to be unobtrusive. You'll find that people will be much more willing to take the time to chat with you if you make it clear that they're under no obligation to do anything for you. Let them know right away that you're just looking for general information, not a job. Who knows? In addition to learning about a potential career path, you may even gain a valuable contact in the process. (For an example of a casual networking letter, see the Resources section at the back of this book.)

The Informational Field Trip: Interview Questions

- Why did you choose this career?
- What's your background/career path?
- Can you give me an example of a typical workday?
- What's the corporate culture like?
- What are your hours?
- How many people do you work with?
- What's the best part about your job? The worst?
- What's the salary range for someone starting out? A veteran?
- What kind of skills and education are necessary for this job?
- What other kinds of careers can this job lead to?
- What would someone be most surprised to learn about your job?

Outside of school, grab any opportunity you can to get practical experience. Offer your services to local stage productions, do some mixing at a church. (Church audio is big business! Skeptical? Check out the Church Sound Education Network at *www.jdbsound.com* or Church Soundcheck Bootcamp at *www.churchsoundcheck.com*.) Volunteer at the local cable station. (Community-access shows are notorious for having the worst audio around.) Any gig you can get your hands on will boost your practical skills. Not only that, but you may even gain something concrete to show for it, like a CD you mixed of a show, or a video production demo reel.

Experience doesn't always have to be in your target field to be relevant or useful: Robert Scovill tells his live sound students at the Conservatory of Recording Arts and Sciences to learn the ropes in a studio before heading out on the road. "It's too hard to learn how to mix on the road; it's too hostile an environment, and there are too many variables. It changes every day," he says. Ex'Pression Center for New Media professor and engineer David Ogilvy says that a year of working in a music store was surprisingly helpful in rounding out his music experience. I'd recommend that for anyone who wants to be an engineer," he says. "Especially if you haven't played in a school band or really been around a lot of different instruments. You need to know types of reeds, different parts of a sax. That's just all good information to have if you're going to be working with musicians. I didn't plan it that way, but it certainly did help. Plus, you get to pick up a lot of jokes."

If you've got the means, you might think about picking up a couple of pieces of cheap gear. For example, Digidesign Pro Tools LE audio editing software is an amazingly powerful tool that just about all engineers use. (To learn how to get the most out of the software, see Mitch Gallagher's *Pro Tools Clinic.*) Another option is to rent some gear. But even if you're broke, you can still get your hands on some audio tools without spending a penny. The Internet is a huge resource for freebies. Plenty of software companies offer limited demo versions of their products for download, and you'd be surprised at how much audio shareware is out there. You can even download a free version of Pro Tools on Digidesign's Website. (Note: I am in no way advocating the use of "kracked" or pirated applications. You need to be aware that there are plenty of talented, creative people just like you out there working hard to create the products that help make your mixes sound great, and stealing software not only chips away at their livelihood, it seriously hurts the chances of more great tools coming from them in the future. And I know I don't have to remind you that it's illegal. Stick to the legit goods!)

The most important way to maximize your time right now is to absorb information like a sponge and apply it as much as you can. The skills and contacts you gain now will largely determine where you go when you venture out into the world for your internship.

"Many people, throughout their entire school career, learn what they need to know to pass the test, for the purposes of passing the test. And once they pass the test, they forget it. Audio students are no exception," says Quad Recording's Bill Ring. "But when these students venture out into the 'real world,' they discover that those things that they were taught and since forgotten are tools they need to know, and they must re-learn skills, this time on the job." So if you can learn to take the theoretical information presented to you in school and relate it to practice, you'll have a better chance of getting ahead in the studio.

"Very few people in this industry, even professional engineers who have been doing it a long time, understand the theoretical reasons for what they do. It's mostly 'press the button and get a banana.' We are trained to do that in this society," continues Ring. "If people would try to learn the theory they're taught in schools with an eye toward what that theory means in terms of doing practical things, once they got into the studio they'd be a million miles ahead of everybody else and they'd probably be the one to get the assistant's job." Remember, your goal is to make yourself as employable as possible, and all of these steps help.

Robert Scovill
Live Sound Engineer

"One of my mottoes is, if you want to be in the right place at the right time, first you have to be in the right place."

Robert Scovill can trace his career back to one fateful Supertramp show. The renowned live sound mixer was just 13 years old when he convinced his mother to take him to his first rock concert. Not long after that, at Supertramp's "Crime of the Century" tour, he realized that the experience was nothing like listening to his records in his bedroom. "Even at that age, all of a sudden it was painfully obvious that there was more going on here than just the musicians up onstage playing," says Scovill. "It sounded so much greater than anything I had heard up to that point, and I remember thinking, 'I gotta know what's going on here! This is unbelievable.'" As he walked past the front-of-house console, he climbed up on the risers and asked the mixer what all the gear was for. "He was very patient and receptive and showed me around, and that was one of the things that set the hook in me early on. From that moment on, I was like, I gotta figure out how to get into this side of the business." In high school, Scovill turned to his guidance counselor for advice on breaking into the industry. "Of course, his response was, 'Oh, to do something technical, you have to join the army,'" he says with a laugh. "I said, 'Let's just start at the beginning again. I'm not joining the army. Now, how do I get into this business?'" It was the mid-1970s, when getting an audio education meant working your way up at a recording studio that was willing to take you in.

Scovill ended up enrolling at Missouri Technical Institute in Kansas City and began working toward a Bachelor's degree in electronic engineering. "I figured, well, it's electronics, you gotta know about that; maybe I'll go get a degree in electronics. Really, I didn't have many choices," he says. He was moonlighting at a recording studio to help pay his way through school and found the benefits of working twofold: While learning the technical fundamentals in class, he gained hands-on audio experience at work. "It was funny. I could walk into these shows and studio gigs and not be able to tell you how the console works, but I could talk to you about how to design one!" he says. In the studio and at local sound companies, Scovill found knowledgeable mentors who helped him build audio skills; on weekends, he took it upon himself to learn the sound reinforcement ropes.

"I remember Superior Sound, a local sound company, would come to the school and put up a flyer looking for help on the weekends," he says. "They were doing this big summer concert series, free concerts that the city sponsored; one week it may be Pat Metheney, one week the Kansas City Philharmonic." Scovill was dying for an in; he headed down to the first concert and asked for the job. "I said, 'Okay, you guys, give me a call. I'd love to work every weekend on this thing,' and they didn't call," he says. "Next weekend comes, and they don't call. Next weekend comes, and they don't call." Growing impatient waiting around, he took matters into his own hands. "I just went down to the park and started working. I would just show up on the site and join in," he explains. "They knew me from the first week I was there; everybody just assumed that I had been called back." By the end of the summer series, Scovill was the foreman on the project. "They had this rotating crew, and I was the only guy that was coming every week!" At the end of the season, he broke the news to the company about his secret scheme. "They said, 'You mean we never called you and you've just been coming here? We never paid you for the whole summer?' " The next thing he knew, he was helping oversee their rental systems—this time, for pay.

At the same time, bands in the studio began asking him to join them on the road, and just six months shy of his degree, he left school to go on tour. "I was working as an all-purpose guy, doing drums, mixing monitors, and I was smart enough to network with every person I could network with," says Scovill. The acts he mixed were opening for larger acts, with bigger touring companies, and his career snowballed from there. Today, Scovill is regarded as a top live-sound engineer, demanded by artists such as Tom Petty, Rush, Matchbox 20, Prince, Foreigner, and Def Leppard, and when he's not on the road, he divides his time between projects for his own record label and studio and teaching at the Conservatory of Recording Arts and Sciences in Arizona. But touring will always remain his first love. "I've spent 25 years of my life in this industry. I really think live performance is the core of our industry. I think music doesn't really work unless you can go out and see it live," he says. "Pretty early on, I had the choice of being in the studio or do the concert thing, and I loved the vulnerability and the excitement of the concert thing. I love the concept that it could just go completely south at any moment. But when it's really great, you know, the nights when it's all fire, and the band's kicking ass, the lighting's great, the sound's great, and the crowd's into it, you take those nights to your grave. It's an awesome experience when that happens."

Scovill attributes his career success to hard work and motivation. "My story alone would lead people to believe that there's such a game of chance, and there's some truth in that," he says. "I could very easily not be in the place I am, had the pieces of the puzzle not fallen into place just right. But one of my mottoes is, 'If you want to be in the right place at the right time, first you have to be in the right place.' You're not going to find it hanging down at the corner; you have to go hang in those circles to get involved—you just do. And if you're in the right place, the right time will come."

CHAPTER THREE

GOING WHERE THE JOBS ARE

Let's talk about making lifestyle and career choices, based on your priorities. Once you've completed your education, you're ready to move into the "real world." For this next step, you need to make a big decision: Do you want to move to an industry center to maximize your job prospects, or would you rather make the most of opportunities right where you are?

It used to be that to make it big in the music business, you had to live in either New York, Los Angeles, or Nashville. Although these cities are still considered industry Meccas, times have changed. Better, more accessible, and cheaper audio and computer developments have really leveled the playing field when it comes to technology. Meaning, there are both more opportunities and more competition everywhere. Which geographical areas best match your career and lifestyle goals? Do you want to go where the job is or find a job where you are? Maybe you prefer the small-town life. How do you build a successful career in a place that may not be a hotbed of audio activity? Do you want to be a big fish in a small pond? There are limitations you'll have to accept. On the other hand, maybe you want to work in the "big league" and you're committed to going where those jobs are, no matter where you have to go. Are you willing to endure high rents and a big-city lifestyle? Know that you do have choices.

MOVING TO A TRADITIONAL MARKET
Although opportunities exist everywhere these days, the majority of jobs are still centered around traditional industry centers. For pop/rock music recording and film production, New York and Los Angeles remain the top markets. If you want to make it big in country or Christian music, Nashville is the place to be. Atlanta and Miami are emerging centers for hip-hop and R&B recording. Philadelphia and

Chicago offer more radio and television commercial work. Atlanta is also a big TV broadcast market, and the theater industry is centered in New York and Chicago. In addition to these centers, most large cities offer more opportunities than smaller cities. You could reason that the more prospects, the better your chances of landing a gig. But moving to a major center won't guarantee you a job. And don't forget, a bigger job pool means stiffer competition. You have to weigh your job dream against your lifestyle dream. Sometimes they'll go hand in hand, but other times you'll have to compromise.

Making a well-informed decision can pay off. Post-production engineer Sara Hughes committed herself to following job opportunities, no matter where they were. She ultimately ended up in Atlanta, but the route there was long and convoluted. "I managed to wrangle a post internship during my last semester and started applying all over the country for jobs in post-production," she explains. "I drove all over the U.S., talking to anyone who would meet with me, trying to network and build contacts. I wasn't interested in moving to California and competing in that job market, so I mainly stuck to the eastern half of the country. After about three months, I found my opportunity with Turner Studios, so I packed up everything I owned once again and drove to Atlanta." She accepted a studio assistant job with the company, found an apartment two days later, and started work the very next day.

BIG CITY, BIG LIFESTYLE CHANGE

There are many considerations when weighing the options associated with living in various areas. First of all, city life is very different from small-town life, and it's not for everyone. If you're considering relocating from a small town to a big city, you might be headed for major culture shock. It's never a good idea to move to an unfamiliar city without at least visiting it first. Ideally, you should spend some quality time checking out the area before you make the commitment to stay.

One way to try a city on for size is to spend a week or two vacationing there. Immerse yourself in the culture, landscape, and noise. But don't just hit the tourist track. Ride public transit, walk the streets, go to "local" restaurants and bars, and see how you feel at the end of your trip. Are you scrambling to catch the next plane out of there, or do you wish you could stay longer? Were you comfortable getting around? How much money did you spend? Better yet, take this plan to the next level: Schedule some informational interviews while you're there.

Perhaps you're still not really sure if the big city is for you. Not ready for, say, New York or Los Angeles? Consider moving to a nearby suburb, or perhaps try out a secondary market like San Francisco or Boston as a "stepping stone" to your goal. Although the cost of living will be roughly the same in those cities as their larger counterparts, they're more compact, less overwhelming places to be.

If you settle down in a primary market, keep a realistic perspective. Don't expect opportunities to be raining down around you, and don't get discouraged if you can't land your dream job right away. Remember that you're not the only one out there looking and if you're new, you'll need to develop the skills and work experience necessary to land the gigs you really want. You may have to consider taking on temporary work or even a second job while you climb your way up the career ladder. Working in this industry takes a lot of perseverance, so hang in there! Have long-term goals, be patient, and work hard.

Quiz: Am I Ready to Move to a Big City?

1. a) I have enough money for six months' rent and groceries in my savings account.
   b) I have a positive balance in my savings account.
   c) What's a savings account?

2. a) Public transit is a networking opportunity.
   b) Public transit is a challenge and adventure.
   c) Public transit is terrifying.

3. a) I can carry a grocery bag, my mail, and a water bottle up three flights of stairs, while chatting on my cell.
   b) I can climb three flights of stairs without much aggravation.
   c) Carry me!

4. a) I love talking to strangers on the street; they're future friends!
   b) I'm not afraid to ask a stranger for directions.
   c) If a stranger asked me what time it is, I'd bolt.

5. a) $4.75 for a gallon of milk? No problem, I'll just top it off with free half-and-halfs from 7-11.
   b) $4.75 for a gallon of milk? Guess I'll have to ration my beer money.
   c) $4.75 for a gallon of milk? What kind of crime is this? Get me the manager.

If you answered…

Mostly a's: Congratulations, overachiever, you're more than ready for the big city. But is it ready for you?

Mostly b's: You have the potential to make a smooth transition, but plan carefully!

Mostly c's: With a little coaxing, you might be able to leave…your parents.

BUILDING A CAREER IN A SECONDARY MARKET

Let's say you don't live anywhere near an industry center, and that's just fine with you. It is possible to tailor a career around your lifestyle in a smaller market; just know that there are fewer obvious opportunities. You'll have to be a little more resourceful. The bright side? There may be fewer opportunities in a secondary market, but there's less competition, too. And with a little creativity, you'll reap the benefits of preserving the lifestyle you want, on your terms.

Sometimes you can uncover a job niche that's been overlooked in your area. Studio owner Sherwin Agard has built a successful business around recording rap and hip-hop in Boston. "People can make jobs where they are," he explains. "In the music business in Boston, everyone's more successful by moving out [to a bigger market]. We're just a few hours from New York, which is a Mecca; but also, we've got Berklee, we've got all these music schools. So in a lot of these places like New York, they're being hatched out of Boston. You can take advantage of that." Agard says part of the reason he's done so well in Boston is, he's picking up a niche market. "The majority of people who come to me are rappers," he says. "My studio is not in the downtown area; all the studios there get all the commercials, the jingles, the people paying big bucks. I'm in the trenches. I had a rapper come in here and she said, 'Is it alright if I swear in here?' I said, 'Yeah!' And she said, 'Some of the studios don't want me to swear.'"

"99.9% of audio work is without glamour," adds Tufts University's Paul Lehrman. "Bread-and-butter audio isn't Madonna and Radiohead and Dr. Dre. It's local furniture-store commercials and high-school death-metal band demos." If you're in a secondary market—or sometimes even in a primary market—you can find lucrative gigs by being proactive. *Mix*'s George Petersen suggests approaching choirs, community bands, school bands, and orchestras and offering to record their concerts. "Your package could include CD duplication, perhaps even artwork," he says. "You could bring in a simple recording rig and record it and then mix it down, and go to them with a package and say, 'Hey, we can press CDs for you, do the artwork for you, and put the whole package together.' The CDs that cost you $1.50 each to make, you sell to the groups for $5 each and propose to them that they can do it as a fundraiser and they can sell them for $10. You make $3.50 per disc based on a minimum order of 1,000. And then it's up to the schools to sell them. If you can go to somebody and propose a program like that, you can actually create your own jobs and your own marketing opportunities. And these aren't the glitzy glamorous type of things, but you can actually make a fair amount of money doing it."

Look for creative ways to get the word out about your services. In addition to being a studio owner, Sherwin Agard is also a successful concert promoter, which he says has taught him the skills he needs to maximize his marketing resources. For example, when he first opened his studio, he launched an aggressive ad campaign, something other studios in Boston weren't doing at the time. "I started with the radio, I did TV ads, cable ads; I flooded the airwaves," he says. "I started getting all kinds of phone calls."

Securing a full-time job in a major recording studio is growing more difficult all the time, and it's a much bigger challenge in small markets. Sometimes the best way to make a living is to diversify; a bunch of freelance projects in different areas can add up to one big salary, and you'll build your network. "Get your maintenance skills up to par, possibly even apprentice with a local tech, so you can find extra work as someone who helps bands install their own studio equipment," says engineer David Ogilvy. "Through that, they may grow to like you and realize that they do need some engineering help, and suddenly you're their house engineer." Ogilvy sets a perfect example of making a living though multitasking: "My career goal has been to be in sound but not live in L.A.," says Ogilvy, who's built a successful career in San Francisco, a secondary market, by making himself a jack of all trades. In addition to working as a recording engineer, he teaches at the Ex'pression College for Digital Arts, writes for various audio trade magazines, records remote broadcasts for a local NPR affiliate, does some audio consulting, and even works as a massage therapist on the side.

Even top pros in major markets take on supplemental work. "You can make a lot of money doing Broadway musicals, but if you do regular New York theater, which can be very exciting theater, I have to say, you will not have that house in the country," admits Broadway sound designer Janet Kalas. "A lot of sound designers I know have another job. A lot of designers I know have a studio that makes money, or they teach. I have another job, too. I'm a scenic artist for film and television. You can make a living in theater in New York, but I feel like you reach a certain age where you think, 'I'm a well-known designer in New York, I'm working a lot, but I'm not making much money.' So you do things to supplement your income in order to finance your theater habit."

You can find success in a secondary market by branching out beyond geographic confines, over the Internet or just through traditional networking contacts. "I have a small commercial production studio in the San Francisco area, and it's a big metropolitan area, but we have found a lot of bread-and-butter-style recording activities that we could do that are extremely lucrative," says George Petersen. "For example, one thing that we got involved with was, we started producing radio shows, documentary shows about life in America that were for Asian broadcast. It was kind of like an 'Entertainment Tonight'-style show about life in America, designed for foreign-language learning. We hired somebody else to write the scripts for these one-hour radio documentaries that were all about life in America. All these shows required us to have was a pair of quality microphones for vocal recording, a 2-track reel-to-reel recorder, a sound-effects library, and a library of copyright-free production music that we could use as background music for the shows. And we also needed the ability to occasionally score small pieces with MIDI. We did these shows for about six years and wound up making about $200 an hour doing them. And this was at a time when there were half-million, three-quarter-million-dollar studios in the San Francisco area that could never make $200 an hour."

REGIONAL CONSIDERATIONS

When you're determining where you want to live, the most immediate concern to you right now is likely economic. You should take a hard look at your finances before packing up and moving, especially if you've earned a few years of student loan payments along with that diploma. Can you afford to eke out an existence in the place you're considering? Will you be able to live while you're looking for a job? (Be realistic here. You could be searching for a long time.) Does the area have a healthy economy? Is the region growing? Understand the local financial climate.

When you're weighing employment options, consider the benefits in the context of their economic surroundings. Jobs offering the same pay in, say, Nashville and New York will support dramatically different qualities of life, due to the size of these cities and their respective costs of living. The same salary that barely funds your corner of a tiny flat with a pack of roommates and a steady diet of ramen noodles and mac and cheese in Manhattan might allow you the luxury of your own apartment, a car, and occasional nights out in Tennessee.

Don't overlook the cultural scene in your potential new home. There should be social activities that match your interests and a community of people your age, with interests in common with yours. Take a look at the city's demographic makeup. How diverse is it? Are you in sync with the political climate (or lack thereof)? If you're outdoorsy, is it easy to take excursions outside the city? Maybe nightlife is your thing. Does the city shut down after midnight? How's the live music scene? Your spirit is crucial to your job success; make sure the local vibe will enhance your wellbeing, not detract from it.

Other factors to consider: How important is the weather? If you move to New York City, for example, there will be days when you have to trudge around in the snow. Are you shivering just thinking about it? If you settle in Nashville, you face summer humidity that will make it seem as if you're swimming across town. And Chicago will bring you the worst of both worlds. Los Angeles, on the other hand, enjoys mostly balmy, sunny days year-round—with a permanent layer of smog. Can you deal with weather extremes? How far are you from family, and does that matter to you? Are you comfortable with the idea of relocating thousands of miles away from your loved ones? Overall, you need to ask yourself: Can I manage to live the lifestyle I desire in this place, or am I willing to adjust my lifestyle to make it there? Moving to a new city can be a grand adventure, or it can be a devastating uprooting. The more carefully you weigh your options, the easier it will be to determine what the right move is for you.

CITY COMPARISON CHART

	Population	Average Winter Temp	Average Summer Temp	Average Number Sunny Days Per Year	Gallon of Gas (Spring 2004)	One-way Subway/Bus Fare	Average Apartment Rent
New York	8,008,278	31	77	212	1.89	2.00	2,788
Los Angeles	3,694,820	58	74	266	2.12	1.25	1,147
Nashville	545,524	36	79	210	1.69	1.50	592
Chicago	2,896,016	22	75	187	1.83	1.75	727
Boston	589,141	29	74	212	1.72	1.25	1,568
San Francisco	776,733	51	59	241	2.20	1.25	1,943
Philadelphia	1,517,550	30	77	284	1.77	1.30	797
Orlando	185,951	59	82	236	1.75	1.25	637
Atlanta	416,474	41	79	218	1.67	1.75	819
Miami	362,470	67	83	255	1.89	1.25	767

Janet Kalas
Theater Sound Designer

"Theater is a great, collaborative form, and it can be very exciting and a lot of fun."

Watching a Broadway show, it's immediately obvious that an immense amount of work goes into every aspect of production; it's a collaborative effort involving dozens of talented professionals, from the director and actors to set, lighting, and costume design. But less "visible" is the sound design: Who creates those audio effects? Who decides where the sound comes from? If it's a top New York show, there's a good chance it's Janet Kalas, who has spent the past two decades in theatrical sound design, working in everything from regional theater to such smash Broadway hits as *Hank Williams: Lost Highway* and the Tony Award-winning *Take Me Out*, enhancing the shows with well-designed sound effects and cues. "I compose with sound rather than music," explains Kalas.

Ironically, Kalas had never intended to work in sound. In fact, she stumbled upon theater by chance as an engineering major in college in the late '70s. "I thought I was going to be some sort of engineer, but I took a theater class for fun—and I had a *lot* of fun!" Realizing the world of drama was her true calling, she immediately changed her major to theater production.

Armed with her theater degree, Kalas headed to the Denver Center for the Performing Arts, known for progressive theater production with cutting-edge technology. She worked there as a construction shop intern, drafting sets and building models—and found out she didn't like the work. Luckily, an unexpected opportunity provided a turning point: "I ended up talking to the guys who did sound for the shows. And one of them said, 'Would you like to run the show?" She went for it, even though she had no audio experience whatsoever: "I was really thrown into the fire, but I was with these great, creative, amazing guys who were experimenting with spatial sound in the theater, playing with dimensional sound, playing with putting speakers in the audience, in the back of the house, in the front of the house, in scenery, stuff like that." Kalas loved it, and the ball was rolling.

Kalas spent that summer in Massachusetts with the Shakespeare and Company theater group, where she honed two skills that she stresses were crucial to her career: "I learned how to make a sound system work and to communicate with people." She returned to her Colorado theater mentors—this time following them to Baltimore, where she fine-tuned her skills and was eventually hired on as sound designer. "This was in 1982, and sound design really wasn't a vocation at all in theater in the early '80s," she explains.

Kalas attributes her career development to work experience. "Frankly, that's the way I learn the best," she says. "I had to learn how to engineer, how to do the basics like hooking up sound systems, how to power speakers, and how to set up a sound system that not only works for the show, but works for the audience as well. I had to learn to record sound effects, voiceovers, and music cues, as well as understand the basics of acoustics, keep up with ever-changing music specs," she says. "The bottom line is, a sound designer for theater has to be very well rounded in all aspects of sound production and design."

Kalas' role in sound-system design depends on the type of theater she's working in. "If it's a little off-Broadway house, or off-off-off-Broadway house, they often have their own equipment; basically, you need to work with what they have," she says. For major productions, she has to configure everything. "And I mean *everything*, from the speaker hangers to the microphone clips to every inch of cable. You're also responsible for the intercom systems, the backstage monitor systems; if you're doing a musical you have to account for the conductor monitors, etc. It's a huge responsibility." For major shows, she'll bring in an assistant to help draft the system, solicit gear bids, and troubleshoot. "While I am not a music composer, I am often called on to choose music for a show, a task I take very seriously," Kalas says. "Music is integral to the mood and movement of a play."

Kalas has many responsibilities over the course of show production. During initial pre-production, she works with the director to determine cues needed, designs, and sends out bids for the sound system and loads it in the theater. "It's kind of like rock & roll at that point," she says. Then, after balancing the system, determining cues, and working with the director and actors in rehearsals, there's an intense tech period when the technical teams perfect cues. "You listen to each sound cue, and build the lighting cues, and you make sure all the scenery transitions work with the lighting and sound and costume changes," Kalas explains. "It's exhausting, but it's also the most exciting time. That's when it's all coming together, really happening." After previews, it's finally show time. "The great thing about theater is, the show opens and my job is basically finished!" she says with a laugh.

Like most audio jobs, theater sound design requires a blend of technical chops, people skills, and adaptability to any scenario. "It's really an all-encompassing thing," Kalas says. "It's not just setting up a system for one band every night, in a different theater; it's knowing how to deal with different theaters, and different shows, and different circumstances, even different cultures; and always, different people. You're setting up relationships all the time."

Factor in the unpredictability of working in a highly ego-driven business and Kalas has to be ready for anything. "There are people who are very drawn to this wacky energy, who can be so abusive at times, but so thrilling at other times. Theater is amazing that way. It's a fascinating field to be in, but you have to really want to do it. You have to really want to be there. But it is a great, collaborative form, and it can be very exciting and a lot of fun."

CHAPTER FOUR

WORKING FOR FREE: THE INTERNSHIP

No matter how much education you have, there is no substitute for experience. In any profession, your real-life learning will happen at work, and this is especially true in the audio industry. It's ironic that most of what you need to know to perform a job, you will end up learning by actually having that job. But the problem is—and you've heard this before—to get a job, you need experience. To gain experience, you need a job. What's the answer to this quandary? The internship.

An internship is a continuation of your education, your next step on your career path. Since you're venturing out into the actual workplace, you're getting your first taste of what it's like to be evaluated on the job rather than in the classroom, and you'll start to get an idea of where you fit in the field. "When you graduate from school, you don't have any idea what your skills are worth in the open market; you need to gain some practical knowledge before you will really know what they're worth," says National Association of Record Industry Professionals president Tess Taylor, who travels internationally lecturing about career development in the music industry. She emphasizes the value of making a good impression as an intern: "Anyone who comes here and volunteers his time with me is first in line for a paying job," she says. "I've seen what they can do and what they're capable of. This substantially reduces the risk to me of hiring the wrong person." And although there is always a chance your internship may lead to employment, at this point, your main goal is to gain experience, so keep that in mind and be strategic about arranging your internship. Look at this as a learning opportunity and plan carefully.

So how does it work? No matter where you end up, this is your chance to spend time in a facility, observing pros in action, learning how work is done "in the real world," while you pitch in by performing chores such as answering the phone, sending packages, picking up lunch, filing, taking notes, and tearing down sessions. Many companies have established their own formal (or informal) internship programs, ranging from full-time paid work to structured projects developed in conjunction with schools. In these cases, your mentor or even your school may regularly evaluate your performance, or they may work together. Other facilities may have no formal program in place at all, requiring you to shape your experience yourself. You might even be their first intern and you'll all learn the process together. (It happened to me!) In any case, you are expected to behave as if you are an actual employee, with professionalism, regardless of whether or not you're getting paid. Remember, the company is giving you an opportunity to observe and learn—not handing you a job. Most importantly, the facility is a business, not a school. They're doing you a favor. It's not enough, however, to walk in and say, "I want to be mentored, I want you to teach me." You also need to have something to offer. Both sides can and should benefit from this relationship. Ideally, you'll develop marketable job skills and great connections (you may even land a gig in the process), and the company will receive some quality assistance in turn.

Film-production sound mixer Arthur Rochester says that he doesn't usually get the opportunity to work with interns, due to union contracts on the movie sets. "However, if someone has the desire and perseverance to hang out and watch without getting in the way, they are welcome," he says. "If the 'intern' is still interested in what we do after watching us work together on the set, it is time for them to pitch in and do something. After a few days, aptitudes start to show. I will slowly offer tasks to be done. Then, I might make suggestions about taking a Pro Tools class or getting into an electronics workshop or whatever. In a majority of cases, specific training follows on-the-job training."

BIG OR SMALL FACILITY?

You'll have to decide whether you want to intern at a large facility or a small one. One of the benefits of interning at a large place is the name-recognition factor, which is always an asset when networking. Engineer David Ogilvy says that interning with Peter Gabriel at his Real World Studios in England kick-started his career back in the States. "After I got Real World on my résumé, the calls started coming in," he says. "I had my pick of many different studios," he explains, adding that he ultimately chose Hyde Street Studios in San Francisco because he admired its legendary history; and he spent many subsequent years there. Engineer Sara Hughes had a similar experience interning at a large post facility: "Although I got a lot more hands-on experience from my smaller internships, studio managers look at 'Emerald Entertainment/Masterfonics' on my résumé and have an 'ooh!' reaction," she says. "It doesn't matter that I did little more than deliver lunches, stock fridges with sodas, and tear down sessions. The name definitely got a gut reaction out of someone who really didn't know a lot more about me." But without the valuable hands-on experience Hughes gained at her smaller internships, the clout of interning at a big-name facility wouldn't have gotten her very far once she made it in the door.

Another benefit of working at a larger facility is that you'll also be exposed to more people, giving you a greater networking opportunity. You might also have opportunities to sit in on a bigger variety of sessions in a multi-room facility that produces, say, audio CDs, DVDs, video projects, and other media than in a small, music-only studio.

Like Sara Hughes, you might not be able to get much hands-on experience at a big facility that's well staffed and booked most of the time. You could pick up a lot more actual gear time in a small facility, even if it doesn't have the status of the famous place. Ultimately, the glamour and name recognition of working at a high-profile company won't help you that much if all you ever get to do all day is fetch Evians for everyone.

Each facility is unique, however, with unique demands on its interns and has to be evaluated on an individual basis. "We have a low 'Windex Factor'—we really use interns," says K.K. Proffitt, owner of JamSync Studios in Nashville. "They sit in on a variety of projects. One time, we did a DVD for somebody and we edited the video and we had an intern who caught a one-frame error, and none of us saw it, except for this one girl. We're firm believers in the young kids in their early 20s having a visual and aural acuity that's certainly missing in older people that brings out odd talents and saves our ass, especially if we're sending out things that have covers on them; they'll catch spelling mistakes that I won't catch," she says. "We also teach kids to solder. A lot of kids come out, they don't know how. I say, 'Look, dude, if you've got a cable that breaks, you're in the middle of a session, you don't have time to run out somewhere, you've gotta learn how to solder.' "

Paid Vs. Unpaid Programs

It's very difficult to find paid internships, but they do exist. They're more common in corporate environments and in large facilities with formal programs that are administered through their human resources departments. Sometimes you can find recording facilities that pay their interns, but don't get your hopes up. It's usually minimum wage or some token amount to ensure the interns will take their work seriously. Boston studio owner Sherwin Agard says that in order to get reliable—and honest—help, he pays his interns: "I couldn't have people working for me for nothing, so I started paying them. When people are doing something for you for nothing, they want something. They feel justified if, say, they took a bunch of blank CDs, saying, 'well, he's getting me for nothing anyway.'" Sherwin says he's one of the few studio owners in Boston who pays interns, and he prides himself on giving them hands-on experience: "I hear about studios where interns paint, bring coffee, answer phones, they don't even get to go in the studio. The ones who do go in the studios do the sessions for free."

If you make payment your prerequisite, however, not only are you severely limiting your options, but if your paycheck is the most important thing to you right now, then you're missing the whole point of this learning experience. And at this point, you can make more money working at the local record store, so you might as well do that instead.

MOVING AND OTHER CONSIDERATIONS

As discussed in the previous chapter, there are pros and cons of working in a major market. Are you considering relocating? An internship can be the perfect trial run in a new city, because the experience is temporary by nature. Or maybe you want to stay where you are, but you'd consider living somewhere else for a short period of time. An option is to gain internship experience in a big market, then take that experience (and all of your new contacts) back home with you. The great thing about an internship is, it is finite, and if you change your mind, you can always move on.

If you've got the means, consider getting more than one internship under your belt to broaden your work experience. My internship at a big rock radio station in Boston, for example, taught me dramatically different technical, business, and etiquette lessons than my experience interning in the corporate headquarters of a workstation manufacturer in California: The day-to-day priorities were different, the hours were opposite—literally, night and day—and the cultural environments were like different planets. But they both helped me develop universal skills, such as using and troubleshooting audio gear, prioritizing tasks in a hectic environment, and working effectively with a variety of personality types.

THE SEARCH PROCESS

The tools required for the internship search are the same as those you would need if you were actually job hunting. Approach it the same way, and employ the same level of professionalism. The skills you hone now are important career-development skills that will come in handy throughout your life. Take this task seriously. Approach the search like it's a part-time job. Set aside specific blocks of time to work and map out a timeline for every step in the preparation process, from drafting and revising your résumé to setting up interviews. This process is going to eat up a lot of your time, so it's best to devise a long-term schedule and really stick with it.

If you haven't done this already, now's a great time to start a career database. It will keep you organized throughout the search process and serve as the foundation of your own career network. Keep track of the names and contact information of everyone you've called or e-mailed, who you've sent résumés to, notes about your conversations, and plans for follow-up steps. Be diligent about keeping detailed notes. Don't rely on your memory to keep track of crucial information! You'll be surprised how often an encounter that might not pan out to anything useful now comes in handy later on down the line. This is a small industry, and people move around. Keep track of your contacts!

If you're aiming for particularly competitive internships, get a jump on other candidates by starting the ball rolling early: Figure out when students at your school traditionally begin the internship search process and start a month or two before then.

One thing you'll realize as soon as you start your search is, you're not going to find audio help-wanted postings in the *New York Times*. And you won't find any listings, at least for entry-level positions, in *Billboard* or *Mix*, either. This is a hidden job market, and you're going to have to rely on your savvy networking skills to find employment throughout your audio career, starting with your internship. It's a highly competitive business, and there will always be many more talented people looking for jobs than there are actual jobs. Audio facilities are well aware of this, so rather than post openings and deal with landslides of potential hires, they usually prefer to go with the convenience and safety of who they know. "Nepotism exists for a reason—it works," explains NARIP's Tess Taylor. "An unknown is a risk, which is why most people prefer to hire someone they know or about whom they can get a recommendation from a reliable third party. Put yourself in the shoes of the employer: It's expensive and risky to hire a new person whose work you don't know, no matter how good he may look on paper. You have to commit valuable resources. It's especially expensive if you end up hiring the *wrong* person, which can cause irreparable damage, not to mention resources of time, money, market position, etcetera." Unfortunately, no matter how talented you are, finding an opportunity often boils down to whom you know. This is why networking is crucial! Talk to everyone. You never know who might have a studio connection. I've made industry contacts in the most unlikely places: On airplanes, at family gatherings—once, camping in Mexico. Engineer David Ogilvy landed an internship at Peter Gabriel's Real World Studios through a friend of his father. Carry business cards with you everywhere you go. Don't be shy about handing them out!

If this all sounds overwhelming to you, start small. The easiest place to begin is with your professors and friends who have graduated. You'll be comfortable asking them for help, they're familiar with your work, and they will be happy to point you in the right direction. If you're confident that they hold you in high regard, both personally and professionally, consider asking them for letters of recommendation.

YOU, ON PAPER: THE RÉSUMÉ

Your résumé is a one-page showcase of your talents and abilities. It's designed as a snapshot, to provide a basic overview of your skills and experience to someone looking for potential employees. Competitive facilities scan through dozens of résumés, even for interns. Statistics show that a hiring manager spends an average of less than ten seconds scanning each résumé, so you want yours to make an impact within that tiny window of opportunity. It's your chance to make a great first impression; make it count.

If you've never put together a résumé, spend some time researching formats and types, and learning the difference between good and bad résumés. There are many job strategy books out there that explain in detail how to put a résumé together. You can find free examples, articles, and other useful materials on career Websites such as *monster.com, careerperfect.com,* Yahoo Hot Jobs, and the *Wall Street Journal's Careerjournal.com.* (Sample résumés can be also be found in the Resources section in the back of this book.) I'll cover the basics here, as they relate to the audio industry.

These days, résumés take many forms. It's always good to have a traditional paper résumé that you can hand out at any time. It's often acceptable to send an e-mail résumé, but make sure your formatting is simple enough to translate. Web résumés offer the extra ability to link to supplemental materials, such as project lists and audio examples. If you've got HTML chops, consider developing all three versions.

When creating your résumé, always keep your audience in mind. This is a single-page summary of your qualifications, so the components should include your name, education, objective, and experience. The more specific you can be, the better. Remember that "who, what, why" journalism rule from school. Take out as much guesswork as possible.

Résumé Anatomy, Top to Bottom

Start with the basics. Place your name at the top, in a larger font size than the one you're using for the rest of your résumé. (Don't go crazy! We're talking sixteen or eighteen points here, not seventy-two.) It should be easy to read your name from a few feet away. Include your most recent contact information; if you currently live at school and you're not sure where you're going to move, perhaps list your parents' (or some other consistent) address. Include your e-mail address and telephone number. (A cell number is best, especially if you'll be moving.)

It's a good idea to follow your contact information with a statement of your objective. Although this isn't a requirement, one clear, succinct sentence describing your goals will show that you are focused, and the person reading your résumé can determine immediately what you're looking for without having to wade through your entire résumé. Use action words and be concise. Customize your objective for each position for which you're applying. For example: "I would like to apply my audio-production skills while learning about the post-production industry by interning at XYZ Productions."

Next, list your education: Work in reverse chronological order, listing your most recent education first and moving backward as you progress down the page. List degrees, certificate programs, and significant seminars and workshops (if you've completed a Pro Tools certification course, for example), including the school name, location, and graduation date or dates attended. Draw the line, however, at high school. Boasting about your job working sound effects in the senior class production of *Grease* is too much information!

The meat of your résumé will outline your experience and skills: A common résumé format combines chronological experience with a summary of qualifications. A summary of qualifications is a chance to highlight your relevant skills right off the bat, before digging into your employment history, which is likely not that strong at this point. Consider this format if you haven't had a lot of relevant work experience (and if you're applying for an internship, you probably haven't), but you've developed strong, quantifiable academic skills. Don't be afraid to focus on specific educational accomplishments. Did you master an SSL 9000 in two semesters? Help with construction of a new tracking room? Talk it up. Another advantage of this section is that it draws attention away from your past experience (especially if you're changing careers), focusing more on your current skill set and goals.

List your experience in reverse chronological order, as well. At this point, you may not have much relevant audio work experience (that's why you're interning, right?), but volunteer projects and schoolwork can make an impact. Say you helped out in studio maintenance work at the school for three semesters—mention it here. If you recorded the music department's fall concert series, describe your involvement. You want to demonstrate your experience on different levels: With technology and equipment, projects, and people. Highlight specific accomplishments. If you wrote databases for scheduling school studio time and automating media inventory as part of your volunteer maintenance work, for example, describe the task—and the results.

List your major work experience, even if your jobs were unrelated to audio. A solid employment history demonstrates fiscal responsibility and strong work ethic, and it shows that you've managed to take charge of your own finances. General skills make you a well-balanced employee, so don't discount those "random jobs": Running a record store, for example, demonstrates experience managing schedules, product inventory, and budgets, plus exposure to a variety of music; coaching a basketball team shows you're a strong motivator and understand the importance of teamwork. Here, you want to highlight your most relevant responsibilities, even if they weren't your primary duties. (But remember, there's a fine line between showcasing your skills and pure exaggeration: Nobody is going to take you seriously if you try to pass off your summer job taking orders at the burger joint drive-thru as "live sound experience.")

And although it's tempting to demonstrate your epic work history by listing every job you've ever had, all the way back to raking leaves and babysitting, remember that the less distracting unrelated content you include, the more impact your relevant information will have.

Include memberships in professional organizations. This shows career commitment and involvement in your professional community. If you held a student officer position or planned any campus events, make sure you include that information.

Including your personal interests is optional. Generally, don't take up useful space for hobbies unless they're relevant to your career focus—for example, if you play in a band or produce short films. Showing that you have hobbies can boost your image as a well-rounded person, but be careful. You never know who will be looking at your résumé and what they'll think of your interests, so it's best to play it safe. Less is more! It's probably a good idea to keep your passions for, say, hunting, Dungeons and Dragons, or your Beanie Baby collection to yourself. In addition, it's assumed that you'll furnish references on request, so adding a line about references on your résumé is also optional.

Create more than one résumé: If you're branching out and targeting a few different fields, such as live sound and post-production, tailor individual résumés to present yourself as meeting the unique needs of these areas. It's more effort to customize your résumé for specific markets, but it's worth it. Warning—don't go overboard! It makes sense to tailor, say, your objective for a specific job, but if you've done your homework and perfected the perfect one-page snapshot of your most marketable skills and accomplishments, why mess with it? The more variables you introduce with cutting and pasting your résumé, the higher potential for confusion and errors. ("Oops, did I send that large touring company my special small-club résumé by mistake?")

Keeping it Clean: Style Tips

You have to pack a lot of information on your résumé, yet it has to be easy to read quickly. A few style tips will help you make the most of the little real estate you have to work with. The idea here is to pack as much information into as few words as possible. Leave some "white space"—that is, have some "air" around your text. A résumé that's as dense as a phone book is a major turnoff. It looks intimidating, and will take too much time to read, upping the chances that you'll lose your audience halfway through. Here, bullet points are more effective than long, wordy paragraphs. Be concise; take out any unnecessary phrases. (Don't worry, it's acceptable to use incomplete sentences in this format.) Listing your accomplishments will have more impact if you include the specific results of your actions.

Consider the following two lines. Which is easier to read?

"I was responsible for maintaining and configuring two tracking rooms as part of my volunteer experience"

or

• maintained and configured two tracking rooms

Now imagine dozens of these lines on a page, and you can see which style will hold the attention of the reader longer.

Use the active voice for stronger effect: "I recorded a concert series," versus "A concert series was recorded by me." Other impact boosters: Use strong action verbs, such as "led," "managed," "initiated," "directed," and "produced." Skip meaningless, tired clichés such as "solutions oriented," or the worst, "I'm a people person." Take the time to come up with original phrases that set you apart. Be specific; qualify your statements as much as possible. "Tracked, mixed, and mastered albums for three rock bands and two string quartets" paints a much more detailed picture than "created five albums." Because you're already so familiar with the details of your own work, it can be difficult to tell when you're leaving out important information. Run your résumé by someone who doesn't know much about your background, to see if they find any holes.

Use technical language, but make sure your résumé still conveys your skills and achievements to someone without an audio background (such as a human resources manager who may be screening applicants). You never know who might be checking out your résumé, and you don't want anyone to get lost in a sea of jargon.

Remember, you may have spent hours fine-tuning your résumé, sweating over every tiny detail, but keep the bigger picture in mind. In the end, this piece of paper may only have a minute to grab the reader, and even then it might receive only a passing glance, so make sure that you maximize your impact. The sooner your reader locks in on something of interest, the more he or she will read.

Finishing Touches

Make sure you read and re-read your résumé for typos, misspellings, and grammatical problems. Run a spell check, but remember that it won't catch everything. For example, if you mistakenly wrote "word" instead of "work," it will miss your goof. Then, have your friends and family read your résumé. A new pair of eyes might not only catch a typo you've glossed over three times, but provide honest, objective feedback. Finally, just like when you're wrapping up a mix, it's always a good idea to take a break from your "finished" résumé. Leave it alone for a few days, then come back with a fresh perspective and give it another look.

You've got a whole lot of background to boil down to one page, so remember to keep it clean. Visually, less is more, and although it's tempting to create some sort of gimmick in an attempt to stand out from the crowd, don't do it. The goal here is ease of readability. For a paper résumé, stick with clean design, traditional fonts (don't mix and match lots of fonts and sizes), and plain paper. Avoid the fussy clutter of curlicued and colored type, patterned backgrounds, and other embellishments. Not only are they distracting from your message, but it may appear as if you're using flashiness to hide something. E-mailed résumés should be formatted in ASCII text. They are usually delivered best in the body of an e-mail, rather than as attachments. Don't apply dazzling type treatment in your e-mail. The chances that it will translate are slim; it's much more likely to show up as garbled gibberish. Just keep everything left-justified and put in an extra line space between each section. If you create an HTML electronic résumé that can be viewed on your own Website, you can link to projects and other relevant information without distracting from your main page. Just make sure your résumé still stands on its own; don't rely on links to supply crucial information.

THE ART OF THE COVER LETTER

When you submit your résumé, always include a cover letter. Your cover letter is as important as your résumé. But while your résumé is designed to be a snapshot of your skills and accomplishments, a cover letter is more of a personal introduction. It's a chance for you to express yourself, demonstrate your communication skills, and announce your specific reasons for reaching out to a particular person or company.

Because your cover letter is a personal introduction, always customize the content. Remember, the company is interested in what you have to offer them, not what they can do for you, so show you're motivated by taking the extra time to tailor your message to demonstrate how you can meet their particular needs. Call to find out the name of the person to whom you should address the letter. You'll show that you cared enough to take the extra time to personalize the letter, and you'll ensure that your résumé makes it to the right person.

Keep the reader's attention by getting to the point right away: "I would like to apply for an internship at Company XYZ." If you are responding to a particular internship posting, mention it here. Same goes if you were referred by someone: Now's the time to bring it up. Then, explain why you want to intern at Company XYZ. Mention what interests you about the company, why you would be a good fit at that particular organization, and most importantly, what you have to offer. You should demonstrate that you've done some research on the company by identifying specific aspects of the business that you're interested in, or highlighting particular areas where you can contribute to that company. (Watch your tone. It's important to project confidence here without coming across as arrogant.) You can also mention specific examples of relevant accomplishments or experience here. However, the cover letter is meant to complement, not duplicate, your résumé, so use it to enhance or summarize the most relevant items to your specific reader, rather than just re-stating everything on the other page.

Conclude by thanking the reader for his or her time, and outlining your next step. The ball is in your court now. Show that you will take the initiative by following up with a phone call within a few days. Companies usually expect you to make the next move. A passive "I look forward to hearing from you" closer could leave you holding your breath forever. Other pointers: Keep the cover letter to one page. And, just like your résumé, check thoroughly and repeatedly for errors in typing or grammar. Remember, you're also showcasing your business communication skills here. Careless mistakes are a reflection of your work habits and could be the deciding factor in disqualifying you as an applicant. (See a sample internship cover letter in the Resources section at the back of this book.)

CONTACTING FACILITIES

Whether you're e-mailing or phoning your potential targets, know how to make an impact. In your e-mail and mail campaigns, be focused and methodical—and use any opportunity to stand out from the crowd. "If I were really interested in a position, I would FedEx or messenger my résumé over to the company and make sure to get it to the decision maker's attention," says Tess Taylor. "Getting it to him by way of FedEx or a messenger lets him know I'm serious." Unless you win the lottery, I wouldn't recommend this method for every letter you send out, but think about extra touches like this for your top choices or the most competitive facilities.

When writing to facilities, follow the cover letter rules mentioned above. State what you're trying to accomplish and what you can offer. Include a simple summary of your achievements, but remember not to brag. Detail any relevant experience, equipment you've used, etc. Keep it short and to-the-point. Put yourself in the shoes of the person on the receiving end: What do they need to know? Nashville studio owner K.K. Proffitt says she weeds through piles of hopeful, yet thoughtless, letters on a weekly basis. "This pompous, arrogant stuff, get rid of it," she says. "Just do a very simple 'I want to learn, this is what I'd like to accomplish' letter, and for God's sake, if you're going to send a résumé, call ahead and find out who you're sending to. Don't send it to 'Mister K.K. Proffitt,' because it goes in the garbage can. I probably throw away three of those a week." She says the same goes for obvious "shotgunned" form emails such as blind-copied "to whom it may concern" letters. To anyone who writes, "call me back," she responds: "Umm, dream on!"

During your search, you're going to have to make some cold calls to facilities. If this sounds worse than a root canal to you, practice on some willing friends. If you're absolutely terrified, make notes about your skills, or even write out a script, to make the phone call easier. (But don't over-rehearse your "lines"; you want to sound natural—like a human being, as opposed to a canned recording.) Don't worry; the process will get smoother and easier with each call. In no time, you'll be pulling it off like a pro.

When you call, try to speak directly to the person in charge of interns. (In many small facilities, this could be the person answering the phone.) If you can't connect with the right person at that time, find out the best time to call back. Remember, you're the one asking for something here, so the ball's in your court. It's your responsibility to follow up. If someone referred you, make sure to bring up his or her name. And hopefully, you've mastered phone etiquette by this point in your life, but remember to be aware of the impression you're making at all times: Be as clear as possible, to ensure the right message gets through to the person on the other end. "When you leave a phone message, make sure you clearly and briefly state your name, the purpose of your call, and your telephone number," advises Tess Taylor. "People who don't, and assume I know who they are or what their issue is about, become my lowest priority. I don't have time to get into their psyches and figure out their reason for calling."

THE INTERVIEW

Interview in person for your internship whenever possible. If you're prepared and rehearsed, a face-to-face conversation will only enhance what you've presented on paper. If the business is local or you have the means to travel to the facility, set up a face-to-face interview. (A long-distance telephone interview is the second-best option.) The interview is about much more than just answering questions. You're showcasing your personality here! It's often said that in an interview, great personality skills can sway a potential employer as much as relevant experience and ability. Strong communication and a professional demeanor can even fill in holes for a spotty résumé, so make a great personal impression. If you're changing vocations, this is your chance to explain why you're making the switch, and how you've prepared for your new career. So use the face-to-face meeting to your advantage.

Pre-interview Research and Preparation

You made it over the first hurdle. You got an interview at your dream facility! Treat this like any "real" job interview. Be prepared: Learn about the company. Study its history and background, recent projects, and top clients. Have some specific questions prepared that show you've done some research, and ask for real information.

Always do your homework in preparation for an interview. Sometimes your research can be as simple as finding out ahead of time whom you'll be meeting. Producer/engineer Jimmy Douglass recently shared a story about a potential intern who showed up for his interview somewhat less than prepared: "I work at the Manhattan Center a lot, and so I asked to be in on the intern take," he explains. "So one day, they bring this kid down, and everything was cool and it was like he had Job Interview 101, and they said, 'Now you ask the guy some questions.' After a while, he's watching me work and he says to me, 'Uh, so, what do *you* do here?' I said, 'I do this; I mix.' 'So, um, you've been doing this long?' I just looked at him." Considering Douglass' long list of credits with such legends as the Rolling Stones, Led Zeppelin, Aretha Franklin, Stevie Wonder, and Hall and Oates, not to mention more recent projects with Aaliyah, Lenny Kravitz, Missy Elliott, and Brandy, it wouldn't have been difficult for the candidate to find something meaningful to talk about, had he done even a few seconds of detective work.

Douglass says that he's also witnessed the opposite phenomenon, where people have walked into his studio knowing every detail about artists he's worked with and all of his album credits. "One time this messenger walked in, and he started telling me all the records I did. He started telling me about this one and that one, and I was like, wow, this guy knows his shit," he says. "And if he wanted a gig, I would give him a gig just based on the fact that he took the time to know all that. And that's really important, because nobody can know everything, [but that kind of knowledge sets you apart from everyone] in that category of people who don't know how to get a job."

It's a good idea to practice interviewing with a friend, even on video if you can, to practice speaking slowly and clearly, and to find out and squash any nervous tics beforehand so they won't detract from your image in the interview. Habits such as hair twirling, hand wringing, and fidgeting are largely unconscious behavior. You may not even realize how much you gnaw on your hangnails until you're caught on tape. It happens to all of us! Once you get over the initial shock at how you appear on video, however, it can be an enlightening experience. Use the opportunity to evaluate your speech, posture, and body language. And although you don't want to rehearse so much that you sound stale, you do need to be ready to confidently discuss your accomplishments, so practice talking about them a few times before you head into the interview. Have a few stories ready that demonstrate how you've used your skills, or have overcome a challenge. It's also helpful to practice by writing down answers to the questions you anticipate, such as, "Tell me about your responsibilities as school studio manager," or, "What was the most challenging part of recording XYZ album?" The process of writing your answers down clarifies your thoughts and serves as a good rehearsal.

Day-of-Interview Do's and Don'ts

Most people in hiring positions were in your shoes at one point, and they'll be gauging your excitement and dedication. So, be prompt. Make sure you have clear directions to the facility, and allow plenty of extra time for traffic, getting lost, etc. If you arrive a few minutes early, you will make a good impression, and you'll have time to collect your thoughts and find your composure. To calm your nerves, take a few deep breaths to relax.

Come equipped. Carry extra copies of your résumé and cover letter, plus letters of recommendation. Bring demo material of your best work. Whether or not the people interviewing you are interested in checking it out, they are sure to be impressed that you were prepared enough to bring it along.

Dress professionally. This doesn't mean maxing out your credit card on a designer suit, and you don't have to abandon all sense of creative expression, but you need to show that you understand the importance of a professional appearance and demeanor. Remember, whether you're interviewing with a major film-production company or a local one-room studio, the facility is a business, and you, as a potential intern, will reflect that business in your image, so you need to demonstrate respect for the company in your sense of professional dress.

On the other hand, creative expression and respectful appearance are not necessarily mutually exclusive. In other words, you probably don't need to go out and dye over your expensive rock-star hair highlights, or swap out your favorite boots with your mom's practical pumps, but you should really think twice about a micro-mini, those "broken-in" jeans from high school, or your favorite "One Tequila, Two Tequila, Three Tequila, FLOOR!" T-shirt. Just use some common sense. Think about the type of message you're sending with your dress and body language, and whether or not that message says, "I take my work and your business seriously."

Day-of-Interview Checklist
- ☐ Résumé
- ☐ Cover Letter
- ☐ Referral Letters
- ☐ Demo Material
- ☐ Business Cards
- ☐ Target Questions
- ☐ Facility Phone Number
- ☐ Directions and Local Map
- ☐ Pen
- ☐ Mints

In the Interview

Overall, just try to act natural. Be conscious of the message your body language sends. Many experts believe that how you say something is more effective than what you're actually saying. You don't have to choreograph your interview performance; just be conscious of simple actions like sitting up straight, making eye contact, and smiling. And make sure you offer a strong handshake—no vice grips, and no limp, "dead fish" hands.

Always keep a positive attitude. Never trash a previous employer or project. You'll give the impression that you have a bad attitude and the interviewer will assume that you'll speak negatively of your next position.

Show interest in the company. In addition to the specific questions you've prepared, ask general questions about the workplace environment and corporate culture. Make sure you don't ask obvious questions that can be easily answered on the company's Website or other public information, because doing so will demonstrate that you didn't bother to do even the simplest research.

In between dazzling the interviewer with tales of your most challenging experiences and elaborate rundowns of your favorite projects, come up for air! Make sure you stop to listen to the interviewer. Nervous talkers often ramble long past they've made their point, in an attempt to fill "dead air." On the other hand, make sure your answers are complete. Interviewers ask open-ended questions to give you an opportunity to explain your accomplishments in detail. Answering with a one-word "yes" or "no" is slamming the door shut on your own great story. Plus, single-word answers are conversational dead ends.

When asked to describe your accomplishments, be honest. Don't overstate your skills. If you've prepared and you're ready for this internship, there should be no need to exaggerate. Remember, this is an entry-level position and you're expected to have entry-level skills. If you embellish, most of the time the person interviewing you will see right through your hype. Your story may even be checked, and if you get caught in a lie, you can kiss that opportunity goodbye. Just be yourself!

Do you need to keep flexible hours so you can make money somewhere else? Address this issue up front. Are you expected to fulfill specific requirements (job duties, minimum hours) in order to receive school credit? Detail your needs. At the same time, make sure you clearly understand what's expected of you in turn, because you never know what kind of requirements the facility might have: Not long after I graduated college, I interviewed for an assistant engineer position at an inner-city recording studio. Our meeting couldn't have been better: I had the skills they needed, we made a great personal connection, and by the end, I got the feeling that I was a shoe-in. I was thrilled when they offered me the position—until they casually mentioned that that they required their employees to have their own cars, because they felt their particular city bus line was too dangerous and they didn't want their staff commuting on it. Vehicle-less, I moped the whole bus ride home and went back to the job search.

Make sure you find out what kind of learning opportunities will be available for you. Don't expect the interviewer to gush over the chance to teach you the ropes, but on the other hand, if he or she seems shifty or uncomfortable answering, or avoids the issue entirely, it could be a sign that you're on your way to becoming an indentured servant.

At the conclusion of the interview, ask about an appropriate time for you to follow-up. This shows your initiative and reinforces your desire to work with Company XYZ. Immediately after the interview, make notes about important points and go home to write a follow up thank-you letter to send out the same day. A thank-you note is common courtesy, as well as another opportunity for you to make a good impression.

Post-Interview Follow-Up

Your interview follow-up demonstrates your motivation and your interest in a position. It's also another chance to stand out in the sea of job seekers. Send a thank-you note right away. (For an example of a thank-you note, see the Resources section in the back of this book.) Show that you appreciate the interviewer taking the time to meet with you. (Don't gush; you don't want to come across as kissing up.) Mention that you'll call to follow up within the agreed-upon time frame. This letter demonstrates your initiative and sense of courtesy, but more importantly, it's a strategic opportunity for you to address or strengthen issues discussed in the interview. Remember, this is a competitive business and you need to maximize every chance to stand out from the competition. It's important to be gracious. Thank the interviewer for his or her time and use the letter to revisit any relevant points from the interview that you can use to your advantage. Use this opportunity to mention any particular skills you think need reinforcement or address any concerns the interviewer may have had about your qualifications. Be specific: "During our discussion, I was impressed by your plans to expand into Web design. My HTML and Java skills would be a great match in that department." Points like this will refresh the reviewer's memory and leave a lasting impression. Make sure you type the letter and mail it out immediately. No matter how laid-back the interview may have felt to you, e-mail and handwritten notes tend to be too casual in this situation. (Handwritten notes, however, can make a big impression and do have their place in business, and I'll discuss those scenarios later.)

Follow up with a phone call at the appropriate time that you determined in the interview. Don't get discouraged if nobody returns your call right away. Remember that busy professionals have a lot on their plates, and bringing in an intern might not be at the top of their list of priorities. Sometimes, especially if the internship is a formal, posted position with many applicants, the selection process can take awhile, so be patient. But you don't want to get lost in the shuffle, either. If a couple of weeks go by and you hear nothing, check in again. Use discretion: The worst thing you can do is hound someone every day. You'll blow your chances immediately.

Learning From Rejection

It's a fact that you'll face rejection throughout your career. You'll be turned down for small projects and big jobs, and you'll need to handle the situation gracefully every time. You may find out that you're not what Company XYZ is looking for in an intern. It's natural to be disappointed, but anger over rejection is destructive. You can either stew and say to yourself, "Well, those fools don't know what they're missing!" and miss out on a chance to find out why they rejected you, or you can turn it into a learning experience and grow from the situation. If you get a chance to speak with your interviewer, ask how you can improve your skills and build experience for next time. Make sure you frame this question in a positive light. In other words, don't say, "Why didn't you choose me?" or "What did I do wrong?" Rather, ask, "Do you have any advice for areas I can improve?" That way, the person won't feel attacked or defensive. People are much more likely to give you honest feedback if they can tell that you respect their advice and sincerely want to hear it and learn from it. Never take professional criticism personally. A suggestion that you need better computer skills, for example, is not a reflection of your qualities as a person! Ultimately, your goal here is to part on a positive note. Leave a positive impression, because in this tiny industry, there's a good chance that you'll run into that person again—maybe he or she is golf buddies with your future boss!

THE FOOT'S IN THE DOOR: THE INTERNSHIP

Congratulations, you landed the perfect internship. Here's where you finally put that book knowledge to use in the real world! Use every minute of this learning experience to your advantage. In an internship situation, knowing the right questions to ask is as important as knowing the answers. Just like in school, you'll only get out of the experience what you put in. The difference between being at school and a job (and you should treat your internship just like a "real" job) is that, in an academic environment, the goal is for as many people as possible to absorb the required information and pass the course. A job situation is more of a weeding-out process, and your goal is to make the cut. "We're not a school, we're a business," explains Quad Recording chief tech Bill Ring. "We provide the opportunity for interns to study the manuals, they can get into the rooms when the rooms aren't being used, they are allowed to do their own little free-time sessions to learn by doing, and they can ask questions, and when we have the time I'll get the interns together and show them how to use a piece of equipment or something." Ring says interns need to be proactive about asking questions and seeking out information. "And that's kind of a selection process, because the text of my sermon when I talk to them is, many are called, but few are chosen," he says. "The ones who are really interested, they're sort of the audio equivalent of gym rats. They hang around all the time and sleep on the couch, and they're always there. Those people who are really interested and are going to go after the information are the ones who are going to be assistants." Ring adds that at his studio, interns often do move up the path to assistant engineer, to engineer. He says there are still limited assistant positions available, however, so there's not much business incentive to pick up the stragglers and make sure everyone's learning. Interns usually end up weeding themselves out. The lesson? Take responsibility for your experience. Remember that your intern mentors are not your professors. The impetus to learn is on you.

Display A Professional Attitude

Treat the internship as if it's a "real" job. Be conscientious and show professionalism at all times, whether you're getting paid peanuts or nothing. Be prompt, show up early, even. There's no excuse for lateness. When time is money, nobody wants to hear about how you missed the bus or misplaced your keys. Don't take extra long breaks. Don't cut out early to catch the early train home. Don't take days off unless you must. The people around you want to be able to count on you, and there's no easier way to build that trust than to just show up. Producer/engineer Jimmy Douglass shares an example of a real-life lesson about professionalism, learned the hard way. "I ran a little school for a while, a three-month course in New York City," he says. "On Saturdays I would come in and have a lab. Each week was on a different thing: Signal processors, the console, the microphones. And I'd end up spending all my time with etiquette. To me, that's where it is. For the final, the students would mix down a song, and the week before, we had a band come in and we'd record the band. On the day of recording the band, people would come waltzing in 15, 20 minutes late and I'd say, 'You can't be here today.' 'What do you mean? It's my class!' 'No, you're the assistant for the day. The band is here; you're not. You're late. We can't use you. Goodbye.' I'm saying, 'You're paying money to find out what it's like in the studio? Well, that's what it's like. You just learned the course.'"

Just like you would in a "real" job, perform each task to the best of your abilities and take assignments, even those that seem trivial, seriously. One studio engineer passes on a legend his boss told him about how he got his first job: "There were three guys going for the same job," he explains. "The hiring guy gave each a 50-foot cable, in a big soundstage, and told each guy to wrap it up and he'd be back in ten minutes. He came back in ten minutes and said to each guy, 'Okay, how'd you wrap this?' and took the rolled cable, took one end and he threw it across the floor. And the first guy's cable landed in a huge mess. The second guy, he hadn't wrapped it properly, same thing. He took my boss' cable, threw it, and it skidded across the floor, went all the way to the other end of the room—and he got the job." Whether this story is the truth or an exaggeration, let it provide two lessons: Approach every project like it's the most important project of your life. And you never know what will impress someone!

Use your internship as an opportunity to showcase your work ethic. This is something that doesn't take years of experience to develop. Be neat in your appearance and your work environment—it shows a sense of pride. If you can't pull yourself together, how can you be trusted to run a session? And as much as this industry is about self-expression, you are representing a business and you're expected to conduct yourself in a professional manner as required by that business. I'm not saying there's anything wrong with multiple facial piercings, for example, but think about your image in the context of your environment. If your style screams "anti-establishment," "sexy," or "I don't care," or in some other way draws inordinate attention to how you look, than you have to accept the fact that your appearance is going to be a liability for some businesses. Depending on which field you enter, there might be situations where you may not be allowed to interface with clients, no matter how skilled, experienced, or talented you are.

Don't make emotional dramas out of business matters. When you first enter a job environment, it's hard not to take work issues personally. It's important to make the distinction early on, to save yourself (and the people around you) a lot of unnecessary grief. For example, if you're not allowed to enter the lounge when the talent is lunching in there, it's not because your boss doesn't like you, it's because it's important for clients to have some privacy. If you're ordered to be quiet on the set, it's not because you're stupid or boring, it's because if you're talking, you're interfering with the work at hand. If the staff complains about your coffee, it's doesn't mean you're a bad person—or that they're trying to sabotage you—it just means you make a nasty brew. This is not to say you have to like everyone around you—you're not there to make new best friends—but you do need to keep a level head and take instructions, advice, and criticism in the context of your work environment.

Remember not to distract from the projects at hand. As fun as your work may seem, it's still a job and time is money. This is not to say you should ignore the talent if they're engaging you in conversation, but don't take the conversation to the next level with another anecdote or joke; any time spent in social discussion is distracting to the engineer.

This may be your first exposure to the art of the schmooze in action. Your technical skills may be a requirement to get you in the door, but personality skills are what will help you move ahead. Be able to talk to anyone and treat every individual with the same degree of respect. Listening—and not just to the audio—is crucial. It's a key part of communication, yet you'd be surprised how many people lack this basic skill. Don't just hear what the other person is saying, understand his needs. Communication skills and appropriate behavior are so important that I've devoted an entire chapter to them. For more workplace survival tips, see Chapter 6, Etiquette: The Do's and Don'ts.

Know Your Place

As an intern, it's important to understand your place in the work hierarchy, and that's at the bottom. It's a privilege for you to be there, and of course you're eager to help and demonstrate your arsenal of skills, but being handy is one thing and being in the way is another. Sometimes the best thing you can do is stay out of the way. Don't hover over people who are trying to get their work done, and don't follow people around. Nobody wants a constant shadow; and if people feel you two steps behind them all day long, you'll only succeed in driving them crazy. No matter where you end up, there will always be crunch times and down times. Know when you're needed, and know when your presence is more of a hindrance than help.

If you're in a studio, never walk into a room in the middle of a session, instead of calling first or knocking. Never touch anything unless you're asked to do so, and never offer your opinions of the talent! Bill Ring of Quad Recording shared the fastest ticket out of his studio: "There were one or two cases where an intern actually made a negative comment on the music that was being produced in the session—to the talent," he says. "That person was fired instantly."

Show enthusiasm for everything you do. Remember, at this point in your career it's much more important to the people around you that you are able to deliver a master across town safely, without dropping it, leaving it in a cab, or getting lost, than to automate a mix on an SSL. You might feel like the work you're being handed is below you, but chances are the people you're working with all started out in your shoes, and they're expecting you to pay your dues, too. Do it cheerfully. You need to show that you're aware of your status as low person on the totem pole, because everyone around you was once in your position. Welcome to the circle of life.

Nobody likes a clock-watcher, especially in a production environment where there's a strong spirit of spending whatever time it takes to get the job done. Show enthusiasm for the project. Put in the hours. Don't be resentful if you're not getting paid. Remember, you're gaining experience, and that's priceless.

Learn By Doing—Even Menial Tasks

You might be shocked to learn that none of your intern assignments seem to tap into your newly-perfected recording and mixing skills. "As far as I know, there's no studio that I've ever heard of who has a professional cleaning staff," says one engineer with a laugh. But while you may not feel like making coffee and running errands are showcasing your audio chops, you *are* gaining invaluable experience just by being around the production process. And that's how you are expected to learn on your internship: By observing and soaking up the experience like a sponge. And although you're no doubt eager to jump in and mix, this is not the time for you to insist on showing everyone how you've mastered Pro Tools or developed the perfect mic placement on kick drum. Post-production engineer Sara Hughes shares an example of an early lesson she learned during one of her internships:

"During the summer before my final semester of college, I managed to talk my way into a highly sought-after internship at one of the biggest studios on Nashville's Music Row," she says. "I was excited because I was sure that meant I would find hundreds of opportunities to sit in on sessions with major-label artists and top-notch engineers working on cutting-edge gear. Imagine my surprise one day when I was handed a tube of cookie dough, a spatula, and instructions on when to bring treats to the in-session clients."

Hughes remembers standing there, utensil in hand, thinking about how, only moments before, she had been invited by one of those clients to sit in on a major tracking session. "I protested the assignment to the studio manager, pointing defiantly in the direction of the main control room and asking why one of the other interns couldn't handle the odious task of baking and serving," she says. "I pointed out that the whole purpose of internships is to give future engineers the opportunity to learn. And that's when the revelation hit me: She *was* giving me a chance to learn, and the lesson being offered was far more important than anything I could have picked up by watching an engineer's hands hovering over a console."

Hughes learned that becoming an engineer required a lot more of her than perfecting her audio chops: "We have to learn how to function in a professional studio environment, how to interact with clients, how to appreciate the little things it takes to make a facility appear as though it functions effortlessly to those who pay for its services," she says. "And, most importantly, we have to learn how to interact with senior staff."

Laura Dore, who places interns at the Conservatory of Recording Arts and Sciences, stresses to students the importance of performing such "insignificant" chores as making coffee and emptying ash trays. "If they can't perform a task on a menial level, like a lot of the big engineers have when they first started out, if they can't pay attention to detail on a very small level, [then they won't inspire confidence in others that they can handle larger tasks]," she says. Think about your attitude in the context of the big picture: The person responsible for a project ultimately wants an assistant who can handle everything involved in that job, from documenting sessions to interfacing with engineers and clients. If you can't handle basic tasks like taking out the garbage, how can you be expected to take on greater responsibilities?

Trebas Institute founder and CEO David Leonard says details make the difference in the studio world: "Years ago, I put on a seminar on careers in audio in New York, and the owner of a major studio came out and sat at the table with the other panelists, and he pulls out a ninety-nine-cent toilet plunger. And he points to it and says, 'We have an SSL console, worth millions of dollars. But this is perhaps the most important piece of technology: The toilet plunger. Because when you're showing Whitney Houston around and there's the potential of getting her to come to use our studio, and the toilets aren't clean, and the ash trays are dirty, what is she going to be thinking about when she's singing a song, and she knows in her heart this is the best take, she'll never do as good a performance again, and then she's going to hear the engineer come over the talkback mic and say, 'I'm sorry, Whitney, can you do it one more time? We have a problem with the console, we didn't fix it right.'" So it's that attitude of professionalism. What distinguishes a world-class studio from a second class or no-class studio is not the equipment, it's the attitude."

In the studio, be conscientious: Set up mic stands, but also refill pens and notepads. Check media stock. Learn to anticipate needs. Be a go-getter. Look for the tasks that nobody likes to do, and do them happily. Find things to do before you're told to do them—even if it's just cleaning up the tape library or updating the client database. Update the inventory *before* it's empty. Dump ash trays and garbage cans *before* they overflow. Performing these tasks before someone notices that they need to be done demonstrates that a) you're willing to pay your dues, and b) you're conscientious and take pride in your work, no matter how insignificant. Use your good judgment, however. Don't take it upon yourself to wire a patchbay, grab petty cash for the lunch order, or install operating system updates without asking permission first!

It's good to ask what you can do to help, but it's even better to try to determine specific needs. "I noticed that there's a pile of cables over there that need repair. Would you like me to fix them?" is a more welcomed (and impressive!) question than, "Is there anything I can do to help? How about now? How about *now*?" Whether or not you drink coffee, learn to make a great pot and find out how people like to drink theirs. In a production environment, you're pretty much guaranteed to be surrounded by a bunch of caffeine addicts and you'll make friends faster if you can serve up a good cup.

If you're working in a recording studio, you'll probably be called upon a lot to pick up lunch for the staff and clients. Don't underestimate the importance of this job! The lunch run is an example of a task that seems insignificant but is actually critical. For starters, it's important to the client, so it's important to your boss, so it should be *very* important to you. As crazy as it may sound, some clients book a session based on what kind of goodies are served at "snack time" and which restaurants are nearby for their break-time take-out feast. And, here are just a few skills you gain by ordering lunch: You'll learn attention to detail, how to interact with clients and the outside world, plus you'll get a chance to network and be part of the team. Getting the lunch order right can actually make or break your internship. "I hear stories where the kid gets sent out for lunch, gets lost, comes back, and these are all studio musicians that are being paid by the hour and they have an hour to eat, the kid comes back with no food," says Laura Dore. "And the client got mad and said, 'We never want to see him here again.'"

Look at your internship as your "first impression," your first chance to really make your mark out there in the real world. Make a positive impact on those around you and, in return, you'll gain great references and hopefully foster the beginnings of a support network that you'll develop throughout your career. You never know, you might even make such a good impression that you get hired on at the facility!

Your goal is for people to think of you favorably, says Dore. "The more people who know you—even if you're the runner at a facility—the better. When a client comes in, if they ask for you by name, even if you're just running errands for them, as long as they know who you are, you're doing a good job. Because one day that assistant in that room might not be there, and they'll say, 'Hey, what about so-and-so?' That happens a lot."

Perseverance Is Key

Making it in this business takes a lot of perseverance in order to withstand the first few years of trying to break in. Engineer David Ogilvy shares an example of a truly dedicated engineer who worked with him at Hyde Street Studios in San Francisco: "There was an engineer who had the reputation that in his first three months there, he only went home twice," he says. "He slept in various places, like in the cabinet at the front desk. He took a shower in the janitor's sink, standing up, with cold water. Don't think there's a limit to it! People really just live, eat, and breathe this stuff."

With luck, you won't have to go that far, but be willing to put in the time. "I truly believe that we live in a society of instant gratification, and in this industry, that's not the way it is. So you have to be patient and pay your dues," says Dore. "I have kids who go out there and say, 'I'm only making $6 an hour,' and I say to them, 'If this is a passion, something that you truly want to do, you'll find a way to make it work.' And I've had students who have lived on beaches and showered in resorts just to make it work for them. We have students that continue to do internship after internship, just to keep the wheel spinning. I tell the kids when they go through the door that the best thing that they have going for them is who they are. If they can prove who they are, and if they're patient—'patient' and 'humble' are the two words we shove down the kids' throats—eventually they will get to show what they know."

When Bad Things Happen to Good Interns

We all know that everyone makes mistakes, but that doesn't sound so comforting when you're the one who's messed up. If you do make a mistake, the first thing to remember is to stay calm and keep your perspective. Chances are, whatever duties you've been assigned as an intern have been relatively minor, so if you did something wrong, it probably won't be the end of the world. But even if you've made a really big mistake—say, you dropped a $5,000 tube mic or misplaced the master tape you were supposed to deliver—your best recourse is always honesty. It's best just to deal with the problem as soon as you realize things went wrong. (Resist that urge to just wait it out and hope nobody notices what went wrong. They will, and when they do, you'll look much worse for trying to cover it up.) Calmly explain the situation, be honest about what happened, and have a solution ready. Minimize the drama: Don't act defensive, place blame, or make excuses. But don't over-apologize, either. Remember, you're being judged on how you handle every situation, and if you can act collected, contain the damage, and be ready to work toward an acceptable solution, you'll make a better impression than if you can't own up to what happened or you blow things out of proportion.

As much as you hope that everyone around you has your best interests in mind, you might run into someone who wants to take advantage of you and your position. You might be assigned to wash an engineer's car, for example, or you might even be blamed for a mistake that wasn't your fault. In these situations, it's important to determine what means the most to you. If the offense is minor and you really feel like the value of the internship warrants taking the hit, then perhaps let it slide. But if it compromises your integrity or could land you in serious trouble (for example, if someone accuses you of stealing something), then by all means speak up. No internship is worth that kind of damage to you or your career. If you can't find a happy resolution, move on.

Getting a Recommendation

As an intern, you've gotten a chance to show off your talents and make a positive impression on the people around you. Quantify these results in a letter of recommendation. This is something you can take away with you to demonstrate the reputation you've earned and show how you've grown. Ask your mentors or supervisors to write a letter for you. Don't wait until the day you need it. Approach them long before you're ready to move on, to allow them to find time in their schedule to construct something meaningful and well thought out. This letter won't be their biggest priority, so don't be offended if they forget about it. You'll probably have to follow up a couple of times. If you get down to the wire, as a last resort, offer to draft something up for them to look over and sign.

You may feel like this is all overkill; after all, it's just an internship, you might say. But you're at a crucial step in your career path. You're learning skills and making connections now that will impact your employment trajectory. How well you perform now will determine where you end up next. You might have prospects at your facility, or you might be referred to an opportunity somewhere else, or you might be seeking it out on your own. But you'll be armed with new experiences, career skills, and some great contacts. Make the most of your experience!

SPOTLIGHT:
Arthur Rochester
Production Sound Mixer
"We are all there to make a director's vision come alive on film."

Arthur Rochester is one of the top production sound mixers in Hollywood, with dozens of movie credits spanning three decades, including *American Graffiti,* 1973's *Invasion of the Body Snatchers, Poltergeist, Say Anything, The Truman Show, About Schmidt,* and *Something's Gotta Give;* plus five Academy Award nominations for his work on such films as *The Conversation, Con Air,* and most recently, *Master and Commander: The Far Side of the World.*

Flip back a few decades, however, and you'll find a young pre-med student in San Francisco, discovering a love of sound through the unlikely route of biology. "I was working on projects for my major advisor, and among other things, he was recording the species-specific songs of birds and then burning them onto strips of paper with a 'Sono-Graph' machine," he explains. "We had miles of tape in the lab from his annual field trips to the Galapagos Islands." The students were then required to transfer the recordings to graphs and analyze them. During this period, Rochester says, he developed an affinity for the tape recorder and what it could do. "There seemed to be a correlation between the genetic information contained in DNA and the information contained on particles of iron oxide found on magnetic tape."

Rochester started to experiment, recording himself and musician friends on weekends, learning audio fundamentals such as microphone placement, tape saturation, and acoustics principles. "This was a diversion from dissecting small animals, viewing their parts through microscopes, and taking copious notes," he says. "Besides, this was the San Francisco Bay area in the mid-'60s, and there was music everywhere. I was picked up and carried away by the wave of free love and rock & roll."

"This was before I had a job, other than being a student teacher for spare change and doing my advisor's bidding in the name of science," Rochester adds. A turning point came when Rochester decided to take a break from school for a while, when he got the opportunity to record dialog and sound effects on an adventure film in Yosemite. It was his first real paying gig outside of the academic environment, and things spiraled from there. "After that project was finished, I found a job at a small commercial production house as an assistant engineer," he says. "My job evolved into recording improvisational comedy sessions on quarter-inch tape and then editing them into thirty-second radio spots for my boss' clients. This was baptism by fire and, luckily, I survived."

Sound became Rochester's life. "When I was not spending long hours with reels of tape, a splicing block, and boxes of razor blades, I was hanging out with friends in local San Francisco Bay area studios picking up tricks of the trade," he says. "Glyn Johns and Wally Heider were my heroes and mentors; it is most helpful to find a patient mentor and become his shadow. I never got any sleep, and my diet sucked." One of Rochester's studio hangouts was Francis Ford Coppola's American Zoetrope film production facility, which was upstairs from Coast Recorders, where he occasionally worked as a freelance engineer. "Somehow, I ended up with George Lucas, recording the dialog on *American Graffiti.* My greatest strength was not knowing what to fear! That was the beginning of the end of studio work and the beginning of a long career as a production sound mixer."

Rochester's job is to capture the dialog and other sounds on location or on a set. There are no "typical" days in Hollywood, but Rochester describes the kinds of events that take place: "Usually, we get to some location at 6:00am—it is only then that I miss working all night in the studio—and turn on the machines to see if everything still works," he says. "That is followed by a trip to the set with my crew and a cup of coffee to work out the day's strategy. From there, the games begin. Whether it is recording dialog on a set or in a moving vehicle of some sort, it is all on-the-spot decisions based on where the cameras and lights are and how many actors are in the scene, etc., etc. We also have to contend with background noises and quiet them as much as possible. There is a considerable amount of creativity in this. It is about teamwork, too. After a while, the set becomes home, while the cast and crew become brothers and sisters. We are all there to make a director's vision come alive on film."

When describing the personal elements necessary for this vocation, Rochester says passion and desire are the main ingredients, followed by aptitude. Other skills are universal: "Common sense is the key to any job," he says. "It is necessary to have respect for the people you are working with and for. Know that they know more than you do and that it is incumbent on you to learn as much as you can, as fast as you can. Learn by watching and then by doing. Keep your mind and your eyes wide open all the time. Never be afraid to experiment or to do something in a new way. That skill set has not changed and will probably never change." Rochester's final words of advice ring true with just about anyone who's made a successful career in audio: "Go do what you are passionate about doing. When you become good at it, the money will follow. And you know you're there when you look forward to waking up every day to the possibility that everything you have learned has changed."

CHAPTER FIVE

MAKING THE CUT: LANDING AN ASSISTANT GIG

Y ou've got the skills down. You've got some experience under your belt. And you're ready to make the transition from an intern to the real deal: An official engineering gig. What should you expect, as far as job responsibilities and money? What's your action plan for making the transition happen? First of all, be ready for opportunity, at any time. Keep your chops up and your eyes open. But don't sit around waiting for a prospect to land in your lap. Be proactive about finding a job: Make a good impression, stay involved in the community, and work those contacts! When you come across an opportunity, follow the same steps outlined in Chapter Four, Working for Free: The Internship. And when you finally do land that gig, take a moment to give yourself a big pat on the back, and then dive right in.

THE TRANSITION FROM INTERN: WHAT NOW?

At first, it might seem as if the only distinction between your internship and your new position as assistant is the fact that you now receive a paycheck. It's important to understand that, unlike in most workplace environments, the hierarchy of responsibility in a creative production environment isn't always clearly defined, and the role of assistant engineer can vary wildly from one facility to the next. It might be up to you to figure out where you fit in the food chain. Don't be surprised if you're still the one making coffee and emptying trash cans! You might be doing many of the same things you did as an intern, except now you have a greater sense of responsibility because you're getting paid to do them. And, the people around you will take notice and see you as an "up-and-coming" engineer and not as a "wannabe."

It's important to remember, however, that you still have to pay your dues. "I could tell any number of stories about studio assistants I've either worked with or had friends work with who let their arrogance get in the way once their internship became a paid job," says one recording engineer. "The transition should be fairly smooth, just greater accountability and greater opportunities. Too often people think that it should automatically grant them bigger and better work. It's not automatic. There's little in this industry that doesn't have to be earned."

THE ASSISTANT'S ROLE

As an assistant engineer, you are the human interface in the session or project. "I tell my students that the job description is this: Runner, diplomat, cheerleader, psychologist, studio employee, assistant to the big dog, and then apprentice engineer last," says CRAS's Kevin Becka. "You're all these things before an apprentice, because all these things build people's confidence in you, and because they'll give you the crappy jobs just to see how you react."

"Every studio has a particular style. I have a style here," says Jane Scobie, manager of Royaltone Studios (Los Angeles), whose client list boasts Christina Aguilera, No Doubt, Blink 182, Metallica, R.E.M, and Alanis Morissette, among other top recording artists. "It's like a small family. We don't have lots and lots of staff members, and our turnover is pretty low. I hand-pick the staff members very carefully, in the sense of them fitting in with us. It's been a very hard, long road to get to where we've got to, and we've got to maintain it. So everyone who comes onboard has to reflect where we're at, in terms of reputation, the way they communicate with clients, because they get a lot of client interaction, and obviously everyone out there is a reflection of my management, to a degree."

This liaison role can take many forms and calls for a variety of skills, depending on which field you end up in. But communication skills are universally required. Broadway sound designer Janet Kalas says not only do her assistants need great drafting skills, programming chops, and a good sense of the equipment available on the market and how it works, but they also have to be able to communicate with everyone in the theater and have a sense of humor ("that's really important!"). And they must be able to make decisions without her. "The assistant is often the liaison between myself and the audio people at the theater, especially if I'm working on another show prior to going into the one that this assistant's working on," she says. "I may not be able to be there when they have questions, so it's really important that they have a good sense of how the show's set up. That's why I think it's important for the assistant to draft the show and set up the equipment list, because then they know the show backwards and forwards in terms of equipment. That way, they can answer questions about cable runs and speaker placement and make compromises, in case I can't be there."

Keep in mind that, while you may have moved up on the totem pole, you still aren't in charge. There are people above you making decisions about what things should be done, when they should be done, and how it should happen. Your job is to implement their plan. Remember that there are many ways to accomplish the same goal, but if you're asked to perform a job in a specific manner, then that's the way you should do it. Even though you all want the same result, this is not your record, or film, or commercial.

Post-production engineer Sara Hughes shares her Golden Rule of Assisting: "The engineer's word is gospel, at least while you're working for him or her. So much of audio production is subjective and preference-oriented, but to the person on whose shoulders the success of a project rests, there's only one way to do things. Live by that, and your senior staff will love you." The happier you make the people around you, the better the chances that you'll eventually get the opportunity to do it *your* way.

Personal dynamics are complicated, especially in business. Now that you've been brought onboard as a "real" team member, it's crucial to understand workplace politics, especially as they relate to your slot in the hierarchy. (This topic is so important that there's an entire chapter dedicated to it, coming up next.)

At some point, you may be established enough that you're in charge, and then you can assert your opinions on how things should work all you want. But for the time being, you're still the newbie, so exercise discretion. "It's funny, the thing that makes a good second engineer is a combination of two disparate forms of personality," says engineer and Ex'Pression instructor David Ogilvy. "One is very gregarious personality, one who's willing to get into conversations and suggest things and not be intimidated easily. But the other aspect is one of a doormouse, one who's very quiet and doesn't let his or her ego get in the way of the session. It's a strange little line to walk." "Asking the right questions is important," adds production sound mixer Arthur Rochester. "Knowing when and how to ask them is also important. The beginning of a career is not the time to openly challenge your guide."

When you're new on the job, take it slow when it comes to being comfortable socially. Until you learn where you're welcome, err on the conservative side when it comes to taking the initiative in the studio. You also have to know when you can walk in a room and when you can't, who you can pal around with and when you have to stand quietly and wait for them to talk to you. "There aren't really any rules; that's why it's so hard to learn," says Quad's Bill Ring. "I'm older than a lot of the engineers, so I can act a different way with the engineers than the kids can. There are certain people you have to be very quiet and deferential with, and there are other people you can kid around and make jokes with. You have to keep your mouth shut at first, watch what's going on, and see what's right and what's wrong. It depends on the individuals."

The entertainment industry is an ego-driven business, and nobody wants to admit that there's a chance they don't know something, so you're going to run into people who talk a good game. And not only might you be dealing with someone who doesn't know what he or she is doing, but you might not even *know* they don't know what they're doing. You'll find that people know less about technology than you'd expect them to—even engineers and people who are regarded as top professionals in the business might have glaring gaps in their knowledge. You'll also discover that engineers who have been in this business a long time may be more fluent in old-school technology and habits; but you might be more fluent on a lot of modern gear (especially workstations and plug-ins) than the person you're assisting. This doesn't mean that the way they work is wrong, so make sure to show respect for what they're doing. Bragging about your Pro Tools chops will get you nowhere.

Demonstrate Skills, Earn Respect

CRAS instructor Kevin Becka stresses the importance of being on time in the studio to his students: "I tell them, if you're early, you're on time. If you're on time, you're late. If you're late, you're fired." This may sound military-style to you, but it's a good practice to adopt. Showing up ten or fifteen extra minutes early is a way to make a great impression, no extra skills required. Engineer David Ogilvy says that putting in that kind of effort enabled him move up the ladder quickly at Hyde Street Studios: "I approached the 8:00 a.m. to 6:00 p.m. shift at Hyde Street like a monk," he says. "I had to get up at 5:30 in the morning to get there on time, getting up in the dark to drive up there and get in before anyone else, cleaning up after the night session, normaling the board, getting the studio turned over to look and smell nice, and be ready for a 9am session. I usually take about 40 minutes to get a room ready, so if there's only an hour, then I'd probably arrive 20 minutes earlier. I'd be emptying ash trays and garbage cans and things that smell, but I was there—there in a studio. Just realize it leads to something else. It's the only way you'll advance. I got compliments for my attention to detail, and I was just using Windex. Just do it! Do everything. It can become a Zen thing. You can even put on music and make it fun."

As an assistant, aim to stay one step ahead of the client's needs, do more than you're asked, and always be looking for things to do, especially when it's slow. I know a story of an intern in a Los Angeles music studio who didn't have any tasks to work on, and he noticed that there was an area near the studio entrance where the tile grout needed cleaning, so he got out some Ajax and a toothbrush and started scrubbing away. It just so happens that Elvis Costello was working in the studio, and the intern was a huge Elvis Costello fan. But he was just the runner, so he wasn't allowed into the sessions. But the engineer came out and saw him working on the floor and asked him what he was doing. He replied, "I'm scrubbing the grout." The engineer said, "Well, when you're done with that, why don't you come in and hang out if you want?" Because of the intern's diligence, the engineer saw that he was dedicated and a hard worker, and gave him the opportunity to learn more. That guy may have only been an intern, but the lesson here applies to assistants, too: You never know when you're going to make a good impression, so always show that you care about your work and take pride in your surroundings.

Anticipate the needs of others. Skywalker Sound's Leslie Ann Jones says one of the most important attributes in an assistant engineer is the ability to pay attention. "Always keep one ear open to whatever is going on, because sometimes you can be the most helpful when you hear that something needs to get done and you take care of it," she says. "A perfect example is if you're in the control room and there's a lot of chatter going on between the engineer and the producer, and the talent's out on the stage, and somebody might be talking about the fact that they're having a little problem with their headphones, and the engineer or producer doesn't always have to turn around to the assistant and say, 'Can you go out and check that person's headphones?' A good assistant would have already heard the conversation and would get up and ask the engineer if they wanted them to go out and check the person's headphones. And they'd be out there with another set of headphones trying to take care of it." Be ready to swap out cables, adjust a gobo, or bring someone a glass of water.

Hone those maintenance skills. You never know who'll need something fixed or when something will break down. Now's a great time to start building your collection of portable tools. The following useful items make up a toolkit to carry around in a small box or bag, and—as long as you know how to use them—will make you look like a pro.

An Engineer's Toolkit
- ☐ Portable soldering iron
- ☐ Solder
- ☐ Needlenose pliers
- ☐ Wire and wire cutters
- ☐ Voltmeter
- ☐ Cable tester
- ☐ Electrical tape
- ☐ Various size screwdrivers
- ☐ Assorted fuse sizes

MAKE YOURSELF INDISPENSABLE

A great way to make yourself a vital part of your surroundings is to become an expert at something that nobody else can do. Start by learning every inch of the lay of the land. "You've got to really learn the building to the point where you know the location and condition of everything in the building," says David Ogilvy. "As an intern or engineer, you often know the answers to a lot of those trivial questions more readily than the owner of the studio or studio manager. You have to make yourself invaluable to the point where they know they can ask you any question and you know the answer."

A technology development equals an opportunity for you to master something new. Maybe your facility just got a slick new piece of gear—along with 300 pages of manuals. It's unlikely that the people above you have the time and energy to absorb that much information, and they'll probably just learn enough to find their way around and perform main operations. Take the chore on yourself: Learn every detail, all of the ins and outs. Master the advanced functions. You could become the house expert in no time, and people will be coming to you for assistance.

Create "new" tasks: Find needs that aren't being met that you can apply your unique skills to. Sometimes this means creating "solutions" for problems the company might not even know it has. Publicity, for example, often falls by the wayside in a busy facility. Here's a great opportunity to make an impact. If you're a good writer, write up a press release about a hot session, or commercial, or concert. (You can find examples online, on industry trade magazine sites, or occasionally on facility Websites.) With your manager's approval, send it out to the media. If you're a bad writer but a great talker, call up the trades and tell them your story. Or perhaps you can get the local paper to do a story on a big project. (One note here: Writers and editors are flooded via phone and e-mail with dozens of potential article pitches daily. It's okay to call to ask how to submit information, but make sure you have a legitimate news angle, or they might not take your call the next time around. I speak from experience!) Maybe you conquered FileMaker Pro while working boring office temp jobs in college. Put those database skills to work by automating inventory or billing. The more ways you can integrate yourself into the business, the better.

At this point, your marketable skills don't end with your mixing chops. If you can engineer as well as the person next to you, but you can also configure a LAN or automate billing or troubleshoot computers, you've got a career edge. If you see a need at your facility that you're not equipped to meet, consider taking a seminar, workshop, or class to broaden your skills. (You might even be able to get your employer to pay for it.) It doesn't take long to learn enough HTML to build the facility a Website, for example. If you've already got those basic programming skills down, master a media application such as Flash or QuickTime, and you can take the site to the next level with dynamic demos and virtual tours. Strengthen your personal package. Learning new skills is investing in your career over the long term.

MASTER THE TECHNOLOGY

Even though today's engineer must be a master of cutting-edge applications such as encoding and encrypting digital files, programming virtual synths, and collaborating over the Internet, the basics are still as important as ever. "What about mic cables? Or how do you troubleshoot a connection? Boy, that's worth its weight in gold—just teaching [assistants] how to patiently start at one end [of a connection] and wind up at the other end," says K.K. Proffitt.

Sometimes it's just a matter of knowing the room, says Jane Scobie. "For instance, today a last-minute thing came up, and one of my most experienced guys—he's been with me for quite a few years now, he came in as a Pro Tools operator—he's in the room, representing the assistant and the Pro Tools operator, because he knows the room so well. I don't need to put an assistant in there with him."

"When you're doing big tracking sessions, you have to have an assistant in there," she adds. "Recording engineers are now freelance, and if they haven't worked in a room before, they rely on the studio assistants to help them work the patchbays and know how the room's set up. I would always want to have a staff assistant in there unless I knew they've worked in the room a lot. I don't want them screwing up anything."

It's important to be conversant in "old school" technologies, because they provide the theoretical foundation that new technology is based on. Plus, newer might mean faster and easier, but it doesn't always mean better. Plenty of top pros still work with "old-fashioned" technology. One engineer told me a story about a situation when a generation gap between engineer and assistant became painfully obvious. "I was working with a famous engineer and we're working in the studio on tape, and he whips out the razor blade to do some editing and the assistant freaked," he said. "He was like, 'You can *cut* tape? What are you doing?' We were as shocked at his attitude as he was at what we were doing." Protect yourself from embarrassing moments like this. Know your basics!

This is a high-tech business, with a lot of jargon floating around. If you can talk technology with the best of them, it'll be easier for you to communicate clearly, and you will earn respect. "Some designers don't know the tech talk, and I think that's a stumbling block," says Janet Kalas. "And then they rely heavily on somebody else to do that thing. But I really like to know exactly what I'm getting, and I like to ask for exactly what I want. So I think the technical, hands-on, hook-up, 'I know when an amplifier is dying' kind of experience is really what's essential for me. Especially as a woman, I think being able to talk to the guys about model numbers and all that stuff really helps, in terms of walking in the door and having them respect you for that."

Have a methodical approach to your work, to avoid careless oversights. This might sound like a no-brainer, but once you get in the session, test your equipment setup. Make sure everything is configured correctly before the session starts, rather than waiting until you're deep into a session, and you're on the clock and the players are waiting, to suddenly find out that something doesn't work.

KEEP THE RIGHT ATTITUDE

It's important to stay positive in the workplace. Learn the value of humility: Never complain, especially at the entry level, because to the facility, you are expendable. And you never know who's going to get wind of your complaints. "Beware of your opinions, because sometimes people will use your opinions to counteract someone else's decision, and you're going to end up pissing off somebody in the client chain.

Diplomacy is the best thing," says JamSync's K.K. Proffitt.

Show enthusiasm for your craft. Boston studio owner Sherwin Agard says that if his assistants don't demonstrate a desire to learn, then they won't cut it in his studio: "I give equipment training videos to every engineer who comes in here; it's mandatory," he says. "It's a test—I know right away if they don't do it, then that's a negative." Take an interest in every project that comes through the door. If you're excited about a client's work, it will help assure that that client returns, and when they return, it'll help assure in turn that you have a job, because clients will often request their favorite person and they'll most likely ask for you.

Your demeanor has a big impact on the client: The more pleasant it is to work with you, the more clients will request you. "I talk to students about how they are the human interface that will make or break a session, because they're basically locked in a windowless room for ten to twelve hours, often with a stranger," says Kevin Becka. "People are tired, there's a lot of money at stake, the clock is ticking, so there's pressure on everybody. The key is being able to function in that environment and make things easier instead of harder for everybody around you."

Sometimes becoming an engineer takes humility, says George Petersen, who shares a tale of the ultimate job-screening process. "I have a friend who's a pretty well-known British engineer, and he really wanted to get a job in a recording studio. This is in the early '70s, and there really weren't a lot of schools where you could study this. But he had really hit the books and learned about electronics and gear; he really wanted a real job as an assistant engineer," he says. "He found out that there was a job available for an assistant engineer at this British studio. The actual title for the job is 'tea boy'—that's what they would call it. He went in and talked to the manager, and the guy said, 'Wow, you seem to know a lot, and we really think you could be pretty good for this job, but unfortunately the only job we have here is scrubbing the toilets." And the guy felt very disheartened by that, but he felt, 'Well, maybe what I should do is take this job.' The manager said, 'Okay, be here Monday morning at nine o' clock, and we'll get you started.' So on Monday, he walks in and says, 'I'm ready to scrub these toilets,' and the manager just starts laughing, and he says, 'Oh, there's no job here for scrubbing toilets. We wanted to hire an assistant engineer to work at our studio, and we were just trying to see if you were motivated or not.'"

LEARN GOOD JUDGMENT

Judgment skills are as important as mixing chops. Learning how to prioritize is important in any profession. Determining which projects are the most important, which are most time-sensitive, and how to juggle many tasks at once is an art form. When you're starting out, however, there's no shame in asking people for help understanding which items take priority, and when. They'll appreciate that you have a sense of urgency about what's most important for them overall, not just what's on your plate that afternoon.

I once heard a great saying: "If you only have a hammer, everything starts to look like a nail." Knowing creative ways to use the many tools at your disposal is crucial to success, and this knowledge comes with experience, so be able to find many solutions to one problem. Know how and when to make judgment calls, and try not to make bad decisions. I am not saying you're not allowed to make mistakes, but a bad decision and a mistake are two different things. A mistake is something you can learn from. For example, if you save the wrong version of a file, that's a mistake. If you decide to join the client in the lounge for vodka body shots, however, that's a bad decision.

As an assistant, you need to walk the line between asking questions to learn, and being a drain on others' time and energy. Producer/engineer Jimmy Douglass admits he holds assistants to high standards. "When I have people who want to get in this business and come and try to work around me, in my mind I believe that I'm not supposed to be teaching you the job. You're supposed to be watching the job and be able to know what the job is, because I was able to do it and I think that you should, too," he says. "The difference is, back in the day there weren't books, there weren't even schools, there wasn't anything. So if I could do it then, and now you have all these books and all this knowledge, you should be able to keep up with me." Douglass says the main quality he looks for in an assistant is "somebody who knows how to shut up and listen. With [my mentor, legendary engineer] Tom Dowd, when I watched him, it became evident why he was doing what he was doing. I never had to ask him a question. I only asked him questions when I got in there and was doing something that was really good, and I had to ask one question that let him know that I was on the level that was worthy. He was happy to answer because he saw that I was in that level where I was computing. I'm very happy to help somebody when they're asking me questions that aren't in a book, that aren't basic 101. But when they ask me questions that are in a book, I'm like, 'You know what? You're wasting my time.' I'm very hard on assistants."

With all of the above cautionary tales, you may be getting a bit depressed about your future in this business. But don't despair. There is a flip side to all of the hard work you're about to put in. You'll be doing what you really want to do! How many people can say that? And, you'll meet a lot of people who are equally passionate about audio and the arts. It's like the last line in the movie *Almost Famous* when William Miller asks Russell, lead singer of Stillwater, "So, what do you love about music?" And Russell replies, "To begin with…*everything*." That's how audiophiles feel about their job and enjoying such company is worth any amount of blood, sweat, and tears.

All in all, there's no magic formula for making this job work. The most important things for you to do at this point are to watch and learn, maintain a positive attitude, and find and build upon your strengths. Start mapping out your long-term goals, and always maintain perspective. It takes time and work to really make it in this industry, and you're on your way!

Roy Jorge first got the audio itch back in high school, playing in bands and tinkering with sound equipment. And although he started out in college as a music major, he found himself drawn toward the technical aspects of audio. He wanted to learn how to design recording gear. So he changed his major to electrical engineering.

After Jorge graduated with an EE degree, he worked as a design engineer for a telecom company. In the office, he developed equipment for voiceover telecommunications. At home, he worked on guitar effects in his spare time. It wasn't long before he was ready to take his equipment designs to the next level. "I was designing music equipment and was getting interested in starting my own business around digital effects," says Jorge. "So I started taking MBA classes, because I wanted to be prepared if I did start a business. I wanted to get a better background." Jorge went as far as designing an actual prototype for a guitar effects pedal. "It started as an undergrad project, and then I developed it further while I was working," he says. "I got someone to design the PC board for me; I gave him all the specs for it, and he laid it out. We had about ten boards that would be ready for production, but the problem was, at that time a major audio company came out with a very similar product—and they had way too many resources—so I decided to finish my MBA."

Jorge says he focused on the audio industry throughout his graduate studies: "I did a lot of research in the music industry, a lot of projects with major companies." He filled gaps in his knowledge by reading music trade magazines and textbooks and enrolling in a recording class at San Francisco State University.

After grad school, Jorge interned at a music start-up, analyzing downloadable music for a searchable database. "We would analyze music using a bunch of parameters so users could really find what they were looking for," he explains. During his internship, he focused his job search on audio companies and finally landed an interview at Dolby, where he now works as a licensing standards and test procedures engineer. What does that long title really mean? "We set up all the standards that any licensees who want to license our technology have to meet from a systems level point of view," he explains. "Say someone wants to build a DVD player and license our technology. We give them all the information they need to design their product to our standards."

After the manufacturer designs the equipment, it sends Dolby a prototype for evaluation for adherence to license specifications. "We hand-hold them in designing their products with our technology," he says. In his support role, Jorge does plenty of testing and listening. "For one project, we took a lot of the most popular DVD players and receivers out there, and we made sure our newest versions of software were compatible with them. We do a lot of listening tests, with actual listening and using test equipment."

Jorge says the best aspect of his career is the ability to expand his knowledge every single day. "I'm learning about what I enjoy doing. I work with audio every day, all day long. For me it's wonderful, it doesn't feel as much like work to me," he says. "If I wasn't working, I'd be doing the same thing." That, and he still has time to play in a band, write songs, and do some home recording.

When asked what helped him land his current job, Jorge says his enthusiasm and interest in the company and in audio in general set him apart. "I was told by managers that [they liked] the fact that I was so interested in Dolby and audio and had the 'big picture' approach—like, this is more than just a job; it's an extension of what I do anyway. That, in combination with my technical background and music background—and I knew a lot about their products before I went in—I think those were key to getting a job. You can never replace the fact that your main passion is music and audio, and that really is an asset for people getting into the industry." Jorge also stresses the importance of always staying focused and working on a long-term career plan. "If you're really passionate about something, just keep going at it. Sooner or later, hopefully, everything will fall into place. And when the opportunity arises, you'll be ready to benefit from it." Jorge is a perfect example of someone making the most of opportunities off the beaten path. "You can find something that relates to what you want to do in places that you wouldn't expect," he says. "There are opportunities beyond music studios."

CHAPTER SIX

ETIQUETTE DO'S AND DON'TS

So, you've got the experience, you've got the know-how. But can you act the part of the pro? Engineering chops are useless without communication skills and professionalism. Dealing effectively with the people around you is so vital in this industry that it gets its own chapter. Here, you'll learn the importance of meeting client needs, no matter now small; how to be a team player and build trust; and how to deal with adversity and exude grace under pressure. Most importantly, you'll learn the value of having a strong work ethic, maintaining your self respect, and knowing your limits in the workplace environment.

ACTING THE PART: YOU'RE A PROFESSIONAL

There are some basic rules that apply no matter where you work. Number one: Be on time! I've stressed this before, but it bears repeating: This is the easiest way to make a good impression. When you think about it, how hard is it to carve an extra ten minutes or so out of each day to get to work a little early? Be polite. Behave. Respect your coworkers and your surroundings. Keep work business at work and home business at home. Turn off that cell phone! "There's one teacher [at CRAS], if a student's cell phone goes off in class, that student is out immediately. It's a good thing, because in the real world, it's rude," says Kevin Becka.

Learn to communicate clearly and *objectively* in the production environment. Evaluating sound is highly subjective, and not only do people all have their own ideas of how a mix should sound, it often seems as if they each have their own language for communicating them. Your "shimmery" might be my "brittle." If that isn't confusing enough, you will find yourself deciphering nebulous phrases like "it's too, um, *digital*," "make it more round," or "blue," or "bumpin." Add the fact that many of the people using these phrases have no idea what they really want in the first place, and pretty soon you've got a scene right out of *Spinal Tap*. As ridiculous as it may seem, situations like this do come up in the studio, and you'll have to be equipped to handle them.

You'll find that sometimes—especially in commercial music production—your clients will come in equipped with just enough technical knowledge to be dangerous. But it's becoming more commonplace these days to encounter professionals who are actually quite technically savvy in the studio. Remember, you must treat all clients with respect. Never talk down to anyone. The last thing you want to do is insult someone's intelligence.

To make a good impression, always act like you have everything under control—even when you don't. Exude self-assuredness, and others will have confidence in you. Remain calm at all times, and don't raise your voice. Your body language sends a message in the workplace. Stand tall to project confidence, and remember to smile at people!

Make sure you're conscious of the image your business wants to project, and whether you're in line with that message. If you interact with clients, then you're a visible representation of the package your company offers, and they need to be confident about your level of professionalism. Of course, this is all relative: If you're mixing front-of-house at a summer festival, you're probably running around in a T-shirt and shorts. If you engineer in a jingle house, maybe it's business casual. If you're doing corporate A/V, you might be in a suit. It all comes down to fitting into your corporate climate. If you feel like you're compromising your sense of expression, just remember that you're being paid to provide a service and represent a business, and you can always make up for your feelings of conformity in your off time.

The audio business is a service industry, and the client is king. Remember that the client is ultimately paying your bills, and never underestimate the value of customer-service skills. "I've been treated so badly on occasion, going into a doctor's office, or another recording studio, and I think wow, if I treated our clients that badly I wouldn't have any," says Nashville studio owner K.K. Proffitt. "Be attentive to what the client wants and don't be rude on the phone, ever." K.K.'s studio, JamSync, has a 24-hour telephone answering policy. "Our phone is forwarded and you'll get one of us on the line 24 hours a day," she says. "We may be asleep, but we'll answer because we really believe in being accessible. Being able to talk to us, for any reason, on any project, is important. We've had people call us from Ireland at three in the morning; our friends in Israel are eight hours ahead of us." Proffitt also stresses the importance of treating all projects with the same sense of importance. "Smaller clients may become bigger clients later on. We've always had that attitude. I don't care what your project is, bring it in and you can do our hourly and we can do business together. It doesn't matter. Treat small clients as well as you've treated the big ones."

"The industry's in a state of flux," says Royaltone's Jane Scobie. "There's a lot of changes going on with the labels out there, which filters down to affecting studio business. The workload isn't as abundant as it used to be, so from a studio standpoint, you have to try harder. You can't give a client any excuse to not come back."

The best way to learn what to do—and what not to do—in a business environment is to spend time observing personal dynamics at work and learn from the pros. Watch how others successfully deal with clients and adopt the practice. You won't be an assistant forever, and you'll deal directly with client issues eventually when you're in the hot seat. For now, hang back in the wings, observe, and take it all in.

Exude a sense of pride in your work. Whether you're conducting a sound check, replacing dialog on a voice-over, or tracking drums, your role is to capture the best performance possible, and that means making your talent comfortable and treating clients with respect. It sounds obvious, but treat each session like it's the most important session in your life. Don't forget that you and the client have the same goal: A quality end result, whether that means a killer demo CD, punchy commercial voice-over, or an amazing-sounding concert.

As an assistant, do everything in your power to make clients comfortable; being pampered is part of what they're paying for. Attend to their every need, no matter how minor or silly or diva-esque it may seem. That could mean anything from providing refreshments to adjusting heat and lighting, scouting out their favorite ice cream, running errands, or sometimes, just leaving them in privacy.

Part of your job is to massage egos, which means being "on" all the time. This is an ego-driven business, and egos are so fragile. Put yourself in the shoes of the clients. The project is the utmost in self-expression; it's their baby. To them, it's a masterpiece, and they're paying you to help realize their grand vision. They're going to be nervous, uncomfortable, and even a little bit vulnerable. Always show interest in the project, no matter how monotonous or silly or terrible you might think it is, or how long it takes to finish. Remember, your job is to capture the sound, not direct the show or make the music. You don't have to like the material you're working on, but you do have to at least act like it's the best thing you've ever heard. If you ever make it into that elite handful of superstar engineers, then perhaps you'll have the luxury of hand-picking your favorite album or film or tour projects, but until then, it's more likely that you'll be working with a wide variety of projects, and there are bound to be plenty that you don't like. Keep your opinions to yourself.

"I seek to get students to check their egos with their coats in the morning, and help their fellow students on their projects, or study in groups and assist others," says UMass Lowell's William Moylan. "In the future, it is not how *they* feel about a recording that matters, but how the *client* feels. Whether or not they like what they are recording, they do their best work—always. The fortunate people in our industry get to work with enormously talented people. Most of us work with people trying to stretch well beyond their abilities and comfort zone, and we can only make great music and great recordings when we allow people to be vulnerable and still be safe."

It doesn't take much for a client to feel like you aren't giving your all to the project: One engineer shares a story about how, after working on an album for almost a year with a famous rock musician known for his fastidiousness in the studio, he made one tiny slip-up and was fired immediately: "I had the system down where the artist did so many different takes of the same song, I had tracksheets pre-made out, and after I'd listen to take 55 of this one particular song—I mean, I wouldn't yawn or go out of the room and make a phone call or anything, I would be sitting there waiting for this take to end—well, I picked up this *Billboard* magazine and I was reading the charts, and he didn't like the fact that I did that and thought I didn't like his music. I was disrespectful, and he had me pulled off the job."

BE A TEAM PLAYER

Just like back when you were an intern, as an assistant you have to always be cognizant of where you fall in the work hierarchy. You might have climbed up a rung, but that doesn't mean you necessarily have more authority. "The problem with doing any kind of audio production, whether you're doing post-production or music or whatever, is it's a team effort," says *Mix*'s George Petersen. "You're part of that team, and you might not be the quarterback—you might be the water boy—and you'd better be ready to accept that." The more you prove yourself, the more clout you'll have. Be patient and don't get discouraged, because your time will come, and then you can tell your assistants all about what it was like back when you were in their shoes.

At some point, everyone has to deal with unpleasant people. These encounters tend to come up a lot more often in the entertainment biz. But the audio industry is a service industry, and part of your job is to get along with everyone. Don't forget that "that jerk at the producer's desk" is paying your salary. Always remain cheerful and poised. Winning them over with charm equals job security. And on a personal level, think of how gratifying it will feel if you don't stoop to the level of some obnoxious client or coworker. Stay above it all, and you'll benefit in the long run.

Your employers are taking a risk when they take you on: They're ultimately responsible for you and your actions, so you need to reassure them that you can do the job and instill confidence in your peers. Trust is a delicate thing; it can take a long time to build up, but it only takes an instant to lose. One wrong move—whether it be contradicting a client, or second-guessing an engineer's judgment in front of a client—and it's over. After all, if it comes down to losing either you or the client—well, you know who'll be gone. You won't have a second chance. Never forget there are scores of talented and hungry people who are ready to take your place, for less money!

"I just say to people, 'It's all up to you,'" says Jane Scobie. "I can give you the opportunities, but it's up to you to take the initiative, to want to get in the room, ask questions, to take control of where your destiny is going. Once you're in the studio, it's your opportunity to shine or not shine, and if I can tell on the first day that it's not working, then you have to go."

A post engineer told me a story about the downfall of a mixer who grew too big for her britches: "Our last assistant came to us with two degrees, a master's in film, and a bachelor's in robotics," she explained. "The idea that anyone doubted her technical skill filled her with open, scoffing incredulity, and she frequently blew off training by mentioning how many computer languages she could program in, as though familiarity with C++ somehow made her automatically fluent on the SSL Avant console. She decided that if the position wouldn't give her the responsibility she wanted, she would just take it." The assistant started developing relationships with clients, coming in and working for them during her off time, doing sessions that they would otherwise have to pay for. "Secretly giving away a studio's services for free is a major no-no. In fact, working with paying clients without clearing it with the studio manager is, in most cases, another major no-no," says the engineer. A project came in that required an edit on a broadcast master for a program that was going to be aired on a national cable network that evening. "She stepped around the full engineers, grabbed the master, said, 'I'll do it,' and headed off to the studios," the engineer continues. "Since she only had two months of actual work experience under her belt, I said, 'Since it's a broadcast master, let's just let an engineer do it, or at least have someone sit in with you while you work.' She was furious. It didn't matter to her that a broadcast master is the most crucial product a broadcasting client can hand over; she felt that the refusal to let her punch in on it constituted grave mistrust. She refused to sit in on the session with me so we could talk about safety measures and working offline, etc; you know, the kind of thing that would have built trust so the next time her inexperience would matter less." Instead, the assistant approached the department coordinator and the department head, saying she felt she was being discriminated against and that no one had the right to question her capability, adding that clients had been letting her work on their projects during her downtime. "The department head said, 'You've been doing *what?*' and invited her to quit or be fired. She was gone in short order."

On the other hand, you're often at the mercy of people who make snap judgments. You may not have the luxury of spending a lot of quality time to make a good impression, so you've got to be on your best behavior all the time. Your talent, experience, and personality are your greatest weapons against adversity in the workplace. If you consistently demonstrate solid skills with a positive attitude, you'll win over even the most hostile adversaries.

When you get the opportunity to participate in a project, do what you're told, in the manner you're told to do it. In other words, the way you learned in school or at your last job isn't always the way that everyone works. There's always more than one approach to achieve the same results, and your way isn't always going to be the best way. You'll find that some of the techniques you encounter in the field seem outdated compared to the methods you learned in the classroom. Don't forget that some of the most respected engineers in this industry grew up with earlier generations of technology and have found that their "old school" techniques still work best for them. Or perhaps they prefer the sound of vintage gear. Or, maybe they're just steadfast in their approach. "I frequently ran setups and teardowns with the studio's resident second engineer," says post engineer Sara Hughes. "He and I repeatedly butted heads over the issue of cable wrapping, because he insisted that all cables had to be coiled right-handed, starting at the female end. I didn't agree: I figured over-under was the same regardless of which hand or which end started. Eventually, he explained that he had a methodology for tossing out cables that he felt was impacted by my left-handed wrapping. He felt my refusal to comply adversely affected the efficiency of his setup, and that in turn adversely affected his ability to perfectly complete the session engineer's setup. Even though I didn't agree that it mattered either way, I decided to do it his way, if only to keep the peace. The effect was almost immediate, and his whole demeanor lifted. Instead of wasting time debating the merits of cable wrapping, he had the time and the inclination to share seconding tips with me, as well as the desire to show me some of the gear I would never otherwise have gotten my hands on." Learn the methods of others, because to them, their way is the right way. You'll make more friends and you might even learn a new way of doing something that they didn't teach you in school.

Your skills and experience got you in the door, but your attitude determines where you go from there. "It's much more important to be a person that people want to work with—because of your attitude and work ethic—than what you know," says CRAS instructor Kevin Becka. "You can always learn how to operate a new piece of software, but people skills ultimately are what will get you work. The people who work all the time are nice people who others love to work with and can trust. They're experts, but the fact that they're good people carries a lot of weight. Especially at the entry level, it becomes really important because you don't have the expertise. I tell my students attitude is ninety-nine percent; what you know is one percent."

It doesn't matter if you're the best engineer in the business if you can't keep the people around you happy and motivated. If it's a chore to be around you, you're going to go nowhere. This dynamic is intense in touring situations: "On the road, you're basically married to 28, 29, 30 people," says live sound mixer Robert Scovill. "You're going to eat three meals a day with them, you're going to work 15 hours a day with them, you're going to ride with them to the next city, you're going to sleep with them. You don't need to be a suck-up, you just need to be a real person." It's not hard to act pleasant. Being a professional means not taking what happens at work personally. If you do, you can lose your objectivity and end up making bad decisions, and if you get sour, you'll turn into a person nobody wants around. Conversely, don't let home issues like a car problem or fight with your significant other affect your attitude in session. Leave your personal problems at the door.

Assistants: Seen, Not Heard

In a recording studio, the "assistants should be seen and not heard" rule is standard. No doubt, you've got a lot of enthusiasm for your new job. And in your eagerness to finally put your mixing chops to use, it's natural to want to share your ideas about how to finesse the project—but this is not your place, yet. "I watched assistant engineers on my projects, and the ones that I liked were always the ones who were moving around like a butler, offering something to drink, cleaning up, in the old days emptying ash trays," says JamSync's K.K. Proffitt. "I'd see assistants fall by the wayside really quickly—a lot of people come out of college not understanding that even though you think you know a lot, nobody wants your opinion on how the mix should go."

What's the best way to stay involved, without becoming a distraction? Don't get in the way in the control room, and stay out of the client area. If you're an assistant, it's better to hang back in the corner than to take up space that's needed by a client or a colleague. In session, listening is the most important thing for you to do at this point. "Knowing is fine, but listening and observing interactions between people is more important," Proffitt explains, "because a lot of times the client will come in, and you won't really know who's in charge, and so if you're an assistant and you start sucking up to the wrong person, that will really piss off the person in charge."

If you're not sure whether you should contribute to a conversation, it's usually best to err on the side of silence. Engineer David Ogilvy tells how, as an intern at Peter Gabriel's Real World Studios, he learned the hard way when to remain quiet. "One day at Real World, Peter Gabriel said, 'Hey, come up and sit at the console.'" he says. "I'd been relegated to the back, and I was really happy to sit up there and see what buttons were being pressed, instead of making tea, which is mostly what I did." The day Ogilvy got to sit at the console, they were working on a piece of music from the soundtrack to the movie *The Last Temptation of Christ*, and the artist and first engineer were trying to return to a certain point in the song. "I thought I knew where it was, and they didn't readily come up with the numbers, so I said 'I think it's at two minutes thirty into the song,'" he says. "The engineer looked a little flustered, and said, 'Oh, I always keep very good numbers,' and went back to where he thought it was. But when I spoke up, Peter turned his attention to me, and was being a gracious host, interested in what I had to say, but of course as I later ascertained, that was dragging his focus away from the session at hand. And the engineer didn't like it at all. I basically shut up at that point, and after that I was relegated to the teapot. I did still get to take in a lot of information and learn things, and watch a few vocal takes from the back of Peter's head, but it wasn't as an illuminating experience as it could have been if I had just shut up and sat at the console."

"You can think you know exactly what's going on and you're helping, but you have to be very careful of showing up the first engineer," continues Ogilvy. "He's supposed to know everything and not have to look to the second engineer for direction. You just have to hope that the engineer's going to get everything, and you're going to watch his back."

Skywalker Sound's Leslie Ann Jones advises that, when you do speak up, use discretion. "When I was assisting, it was a very fine line between when you should say something and when you shouldn't, but what I ended up learning was, somebody would really appreciate that I said something because maybe they weren't necessarily paying attention," she says. "But I also wouldn't announce it in the room. I would walk over to the engineer and whisper in his ear and say, 'You know, the guitar sounds a little out of tune to me,' because I would want the engineer to be the one to say that. It's not my job to stand up and say, 'This guitar is out of tune.' I would want the engineer or producer to have that opportunity. This is not really about me; it's really about the end product. And if the engineer chooses to be the one who says that, and everybody says, 'Oh great! Isn't it wonderful that he knew that?' well, you're still contributing. You'd be surprised how that turns into, 'Leslie had a great suggestion; she thinks you're a little out of tune.'"

Some of the Skywalker sessions can involve twenty people in the control room, which can turn into a pretty hectic scene, "and there's stuff that needs to get gone, and you just do it and don't make a big deal out of it, and just end up sitting in the background again until the next thing needs to get done," says Jones, who believes that everyone learns in time when to speak up. "The assistants who have been with me for a very long time, I expect them if they think that something's out of tune, or if they hear a mistake or if they hear stage noise or something like that, to speak up about it, because they're trained to listen very well. I wouldn't expect them not to say something because they don't think it's their job."

"I always tell the staff, if there's a problem with the client, and they're not happy, then they've got to let me know, because sometimes I can defuse things before they get out of control," says Jane Scobie. "If you can, it's really best to nip it in the bud as fast as possible. Because it can brew. For instance, we've got a vintage Neve 8078. Now, it's a 30-year old console, and it wasn't designed to last 30 years. It's a very respected console, but we have to constantly do upgrades on it, swapping switches out, and things like that, and occasionally you're going to get a noisy channel, and if the client isn't used to the room and they're feeling insecure for some reason, then they can use that as a vehicle to complain about the studio.

"We had a client recently who was used to working at another studio, and the band wanted to work somewhere different because it was a new album and they wanted to have a different energy about it," Scobie says. "And there were a few things going on with the console on the setup day, the way that the engineer/producer was approaching his setup, getting sounds and so forth. Something was said that was misconstrued, and it kind of gave them the feeling that things weren't being taken care of technically. Those are the sort of things that need to be addressed immediately, because otherwise what they'll do is, they'll start to feel insecure about the console; they'll think that every pot's noisy, that every channel's going to do the same thing, but that's not necessarily true."

There are many ways you can contribute to a session without disrupting the conversation. Pay attention to what's happening around you and try to anticipate needs. It goes back to the "good assistants are like butlers" theory: If you hear the singer complaining that her headphones are broken, don't wait for someone to tell you to bring her a new pair. Jump on it. If she says she's thirsty, grab a glass of water before someone has to stop the session to ask you to fetch it.

ETHICS IN THE WORKPLACE

You'll be dealing with sticky situations throughout your career, and the more prepared you are to handle them, the better you'll react. When a client requests something that you feel is unreasonable or detrimental to the project, you need to draw upon your good judgment to determine the best course of action. Do you process the request literally? Do you pretend to follow the instructions? Or do you flat out refuse the request? Think about how you might handle the scenarios presented below. There's no correct solution here; the answer really depends on the situation.

I once heard a great job description that applies perfectly to the assistant engineer's role: "Your job is to keep the client from digging his own grave. If he insists, grab a shovel and help him." As an engineer, you're supposed to be the technical guide. But sometimes a client has an idea in his or her head about the way the session should go, and is adamant about it. You've got to find a way to make that client feel like he or she is being taken seriously, without compromising the session. Sometimes the situation takes a little finessing.

"The old adage says that the client is always right," says New York recording engineer Leonard Hospidor. "Well, when working with some young advertising account executives, that's not always the case. But, you have to make that person feel like he or she knows what's going on. Recently, during a mix for a radio spot, the producer told me that the tempo was too loud. I calmly spun some dials—making absolutely no change in the mix—and replayed the take. This time the exec told me it sounded perfect. Always accommodate the client, even if that means pulling the wool over his eyes a bit." Another engineer told me a story about a similar situation with a producer who insisted the music be "an octave faster." Rather than laugh it off or explain to him that that was an impossible feat, he sped the jingle up a little on playback, and the producer was happy.

Here's a sticky scenario: It's six hours into the session, and the guitarist just laid down a track that's so out of tune that every cat in the neighborhood is howling. He thinks it's a masterpiece: The real keeper. And then he asks you what you think. You've got a couple of options here: Do you tell him the performance was terrible? Or do you gush that it was perfect? Fortunately for you, the answer is, leave it to the producer to make these decisions. If you're really put on the spot, however, you could always request one more take due to some mysterious "noise on the track," or get a second take "for effect." But if there are serious problems with a track and the decision falls on you, you'll have to speak up. (You don't want the client figuring out the problem two weeks after the project is finished, and coming back to blame you for allowing such a terrible track to go on the album.) Judge each situation on a case-by-case basis.

Even the best engineers make mistakes, and in most cases, it's best to be truthful. Perhaps you forgot to hit Record on a killer take; you could easily claim the track was distorted or noisy. But if you, say, threw the master away by mistake, you'll have to come clean. And always remember that if you get caught in a lie, trust in you will be destroyed.

Then there might be rare occasions when you suddenly find yourself the scapegoat for a higher-up's mistake. If this happens, take a step back and think: Is the success of the project contingent on saving the engineer or producer's reputation? Look at the big picture, says CRAS instructor Kevin Becka, who says he once made the right move by taking the blame for someone else's blunder. "The engineer made a horrible mistake. He erased the track," he says. "I was the assistant, so I took the rap for it so he wouldn't look stupid. It's a total judgment call. You have to think, is it going to benefit me, or is it going to hurt me?"

Broadway sound designer Janet Kalas says that since theater is a high-pressure environment with a lot of egos at stake, you have to remain level-headed at all times. "Situations can come up in a split second," she says, "where the director snaps and he starts laying in on you, and you don't know what happened but all of the sudden you're the scapegoat. Having somebody with a clear head to say, 'Well, actually what's happening here is this, this, and *this*, and *this* is what needs to happen and it will be finished, and we'll have it ready to go at this time,' that's a real skill that most collaborative artists need to learn; just to gain trust, really."

CROSSING THE LINE

There will be times when you find yourself in situations that not only compromise your ethics, they could get you in deep trouble. Know where you draw the line. "I like to play the 'lose your job' game with my students," says Kevin Becka. "A friend asks you to get an autograph of an artist you're working with in the studio. Do you do it? No! Do you hand the producer a CD of your songs and ask them to listen to it? No. That's not why you're there."

Back in the '70s, it was common practice for assistants to make copies of tapes, to listen to tracks at home or in their car, but in the age of Internet piracy, album leaks from the source—the studio—are a major threat to artists. (Think about the stories you've heard about songs that have appeared on the Web long before they were released, or unpublished "demo" versions of songs that surfaced on eBay and other sites.) The problem stems from an unscrupulous minority, but just remember that an innocent mistake such as burning a CD of the mix without permission can cost you your job. And if it lands in the public domain, you can be sued.

A certain amount of thick skin is necessary to work in this business. "Assistants are in there representing the studio and supporting the client," says Jane Scobie. "They can be put through a lot of stress if things aren't going right and the engineer's not being very pleasant to them. It does happen; sometimes the engineers can take out their frustrations on the studio assistant, which is not good, so they have to insulate themselves from it the best they can." There's a difference, however, between dealing with personality conflicts and taking abuse. Refuse to tolerate verbal abuse in the workplace. If this happens to you, put a stop to it immediately. I'm not saying get in a screaming match in front of a client, but at some point, self-respect dictates that you call people on their behavior, whether that means pulling someone aside in a session or speaking to him or her at a later time. It's always best to act calm and poised when handling these situations. It can help deflect the "problem" back to the other person, and others will respect your professionalism. "If you permit someone to yell at you, you've given them tacit permission to disrespect you," says NARIP's Tess Taylor. "If you don't have the self-respect and courage to stand up for yourself, why should anyone else respect you?" Plus, she adds, the situation is a microcosm of a macrocosm: "If you can't manage and resolve a situation like that [someone yelling at you], are you someone who can eventually run a company and be any good at it? Are you someone who can manage other people?"

Know the difference between unpleasant work and unethical work. You might be assigned a highly disagreeable task, but it might not be something that compromises your morals. Take, for example, the great New York City blackout of 2003. At legendary Electric Lady studios in Manhattan, the basement filled up with raw sewage when their power went out. Since their one-of-a-kind purple SSL console was threatened, they sent the interns down to haul buckets of sewage out onto the street. I've heard stories of assistants who had to do everything from building chicken coops to buying underwear for the artist, as part of their gig. These tasks range from mildly unsavory to downright nasty, but nobody's ethics were compromised in the process.

On the other hand, you might encounter situations that make you uncomfortable, or offend you. "I had to work through sessions where clients sat behind me and described their wives as philandering whores. I had coworkers who'd been physically intimidated by producers," one post-production engineer told me. Only you can decide where you draw the line in the workplace. But you should prepare yourself for the worst-case scenario, because a time may come when you're pushed to the limit in the workplace. It's one thing to deal with annoyances and frustration, but it's another to deal with abuse, humiliation, or anything that goes against your morals. It's never okay to compromise your values for the sake of a job. Set limits and stick by your principles.

It doesn't matter what your stance is on drug use, if you're asked to deliver or are offered drugs in a work environment, avoid getting involved, even if it means losing your job. "It comes down to this: If they get busted, they're going to point the finger at you," says one studio engineer. "And what do you gain from that? You go to jail. Ultimately you're going to lose a lot more."

Even if your job's not at risk, you could easily end up in a very uncomfortable or even threatening situation. One Los Angeles studio engineer shares a lesson he learned in the beginning of his career, back in the early '80s: "One time, I did drugs in the studio with a client. He was a rock star who was in the studio for a long time, and he had this ex-con guy hanging around—he'd get girls for him and they always had cocaine going on—they offered it to me, and I took it. So after a while, it just seemed to be the thing that they had out and I would just do it, and this ex-con guy got really upset and said I was doing drugs, and I wasn't doing my job, and the guy got in my face. He was really pissed off. The engineer was cool with it, and I didn't get fired, but it was really embarrassing and I told myself, 'Never again.'"

The production environment is teeming with strong, creative personalities, which has its advantages and disadvantages. The secret to working well with the people around you is to remain calm, poised, objective, and respectful toward others. Ultimately, however, you have yourself to answer to. No job is more important than your own wellbeing. So stick to your principles, be true to yourself, and you'll be much happier in the long run.

K.K. Proffitt
Owner/Producer, JamSync Studios

"It's been a total struggle. I never knew how far it would get and how much control I wanted."

Reflecting on the career twists and turns that led to her success, K.K. Proffitt admits she's had to overcome challenges on many levels: "It's been a total struggle, wanting to please my parents, as a good Southern girl should, and wanting to do my own thing. I never knew how far it would get and how much control I wanted." Proffitt embarked on a fledgling audio career at age nine. "I finally conned my parents into getting me a guitar, and I immediately changed the strings because I was left handed," she says. "The next year, I saw a little tiny red reel-to-reel tape deck in the back of a magazine and I conned my mother into getting that for me. I still have it; it was horrible!" Like many of her veteran colleagues, Proffitt learned the basics by recording herself singing and playing. "More importantly, I recorded the Beatles on Ed Sullivan when I was ten. That was my first session," she says.

Fast-forward to college, when Proffitt's recording career took a back seat to a pre-med molecular biology track at Vanderbilt University. "I wanted to just sing and play guitar, and this guy offered me a part in a band, and my mother said, 'If you take that, we are going to pull you out of Vanderbilt.' I wanted to please my parents, so I said, 'Okay, I'll be a doctor.' By senior year I said, 'Forget this doctor stuff!' I was always really good in math and science, just loved it, but I didn't love it enough to be a doctor. So I graduated in French. It really ticked my parents off." After graduation, Proffitt pursued graduate school at the University of Tennessee, this time in experimental psychology. But somewhere between playing in local clubs, examining parallels between EQ curves and population density statistics, delving into the new science of computer programming, and working on a dissertation on the relationship between foreign language learning and musical ability, she decided to tour with a rock band. "I dragged my dissertation around with me, and about ten years later I said, 'I'm never going to write this,'" she says. She soon ended up in Boston, and in 1979 found herself at Berklee College of Music, where she rounded out her education with six semesters of jazz studies. About the same time, she started getting interested in synthesizers; in the studio, she became known as "the chick who could hook all the cheap Japanese stuff together."

Proffitt spent most of the '80s putting out records on her own label, Pica Records. "And finally, around 1986 or 1987 I said, 'Boy, this is a terrible business; I think I'll go get a degree in computer programming.'" She found programming to be a practical, if not exactly thrilling, skill to master. "I learned, God, anything is better than engineering software. To me, it's the most boring thing in the world, but it did give me the ability to talk with people now when I beta test, and I understand the idea of the architecture of computers." On the music biz side, life was good. Proffitt was finishing up her latest album, and her band, Bells and Whistles, was on the verge of hitting the big time. But changes were on the horizon: "Dan Ackroyd decided to take my bass player and drummer on tour opening Hard Rock Cafes. Also, I found out I was pregnant with twins," she says. It seemed like a good time to stay home and focus on studio work for a while.

Later, she was divorced and took the twins back to Nashville. Although there was a healthy studio scene in Music City, she had no illusions about the challenges ahead. "I knew that when I came back here I was going to be starting all over again, and I knew that there weren't going to be any women engineers to speak of, so it'd be really rough." She soon met her future studio partner (and husband) Joel Silverman, and together they decided to make a bold move: Open a new studio on Nashville's legendary Music Row. But rather than join the ranks of large multimillion-dollar music facilities, they had a different plan. "I told Joel it would be hard to open this thing on Music Row, and he said, 'Well, why don't we do the first surround studio?'" she says. It was the mid-'90s, home theater was finally coming of age, DVD and HDTV with its Dolby Digital audio spec were on the verge of becoming household names, and the pair was ready to jump in. They opened JamSync Studios in 1998 and haven't looked back. Their credits include projects with Tim McGraw, the Nashville Regional Transit Authority, and post for the movie *Dodge City: A Spaghetto Western*, starring Isaac Hayes.

"When I saw that the 'music business' was going away a few years ago, I told Joel, 'We have to get into DVDs, because it's going to go hand in hand with surround mixing,'" says Proffitt. "We saw that that was the way to go, to be able to fit audio and video into any format, streaming, it doesn't matter—to be able to be aware of all formats. We don't see it as a music business anymore; we see it as a creative content business."

CHAPTER SEVEN

STAYING ON TOP OF YOUR GAME

So you made it. You got your foot in the door, you've proven yourself, and you landed the gig. But being an assistant isn't a career, it's the start of a career. The story doesn't end here. What's the next step? You are just embarking on your path. How do you take your job to the next level? A long-term outlook is key to success. Any career plan should include strategies for building both job skills and experience, while developing a professional network. Let's go over the tools you'll need to stay on top of technology, broaden your skill set, grow in your community, and take a look at resources to help you get ahead.

NETWORKING EQUALS NETTING JOBS

So, who *do* you know? Throughout your career, you should be cultivating your personal network by constantly maintaining and building upon that career database you read about earlier in this book, recording names, contact information, events, personal data, and important conversations. Remember the names of everyone you meet. You'd be surprised how often you'll encounter the same people in this small industry.

It's important to keep organized records so you can easily access information in an instant, and to jog your memory when you draw a blank. In an industry that's becoming more fragmented all the time with the explosion of home studios, it's more important than ever to stay involved with your community. Be proactive about maintaining relationships with people in your network. Don't just wait for someone to reach out to you; call or write your contacts from time to time, find out how they're doing, what kind of projects they're working on, who they're working with. Check to see if their contact information is still current, etc. It's important to stay informed and in touch.

Networking lets you tap into the resources around you—the experience of others. It's okay to ask those more seasoned than you for advice—or if you have an established relationship—job leads. Generally, people in this industry are very approachable and will most likely listen to what you have to say, as long as they don't feel like you're wasting their time. When you're looking for information, make sure you are clear that you're not asking for a job and there is no obligation from the person on the receiving end. Don't feel awkward about soliciting advice. You might feel like you're imposing, but most people feel good about helping those coming up in the industry and are glad to lend a hand. Above all, always maintain positive relationships with everyone you do business with, from your new boss to your old coworkers to your landlord to your pizza guy.

If you're shy about mingling, an easy way to drive conversation is to get the other person to talk about him/herself. "People love to talk about themselves: It's their favorite topic, the one that they're most familiar with," says NARIP founder Tess Taylor. "It's an especially effective technique—especially if you're shy—to ask questions. This shows the person that you are interested in his opinions and/or experience. It's flattering and it takes the burden of conversation off you."

This might sound Emily Post-like, but if somebody takes the time to help you out, write him or her a thank you note—as in, hand-write. In the age of impersonal e-mails, sending a handwritten note shows that you're grateful for someone's help and are willing to make the extra effort to make your message personal. You'll make people feel appreciated and they'll remember you for it. (There are sample networking and thank-you letters in the Resources section in the back of this book.)

GET OUT THERE, GET INVOLVED

There are plenty of ways to boost your exposure in the community. Get out and catch as much live music as possible. Find some good bands and offer free production services. Not only will they be a mouthpiece for your talents, if they eventually make it big and land a nice production budget, they'll probably turn to you first.

If you've been cruising around AES and NAMM shows, you already know that conventions are great places to keep up with technology, check in with colleagues, and go to some cool parties in the process (and to snag free T-shirts and guitar picks). Next time, consider taking a more active role, such as speaking on a panel or getting involved with a convention event. If you're active in regional association chapters, take it to the next level—host an event where you work. It's a great way to learn while giving the facility valuable exposure in the local audio community.

Keep in touch with your alma mater. You can maintain relationships with the educators there, take advantage of alumni services, and maybe even return some good karma by helping out students just embarking on their careers. Who knows, you might need your own assistant somewhere down the line!

Everybody has special skills. Find out what's unique about the people in your community and pool resources. "I have 'go-to' colleagues who I can call with questions; specific Pro Tools plug-in experts, Logic experts, electrical experts, DJ experts, programming experts," says Berklee's Stephen Webber. " In return, I act as a 'go-to' person for them in areas where I have more experience."

Be ready to showcase your talents at any time. You might strike up a conversation with someone at the supermarket or a local high-school football game who could use your services, or know someone who does. Always carry business cards. Many engineers carry business-card-size CD-ROMs featuring their work. Keep your résumé up-to-date at all times, even when you're happily employed. This document sums you up in a page and is a useful networking tool. Plus, you never know when you might stumble across an unexpected job opportunity, and you want to be prepared.

CONTINUING YOUR EDUCATION, AVOIDING COMPLACENCY

Even the seasoned veterans will tell you that it's a constant challenge for them to stay on top of their careers and they're still learning all the time. Technology changes so fast in this industry that, by the time you finally master something, it's often on its way to being obsolete. You can never really be 100% confident that you know everything there is to know about what you're doing; anyone who runs a business will tell you that complacency is the key to failure.

Make sure to keep an eye on the big picture. Sometimes the best way to keep tabs on the market is to look to clients—ask them what their needs are. Watch for trends. Do constant research. Maybe even try some advertising of your various services—be open to diversification. Take a look at successful businesses around you —see what makes them thrive. If you say to yourself, "I'm in the music business and all I'm going to do is record rock bands," well, you may be one of the few who are lucky enough to do that, but it's more likely that you're going to end up severely limiting your options, especially if you take this attitude early on in your career.

If you feel like you're "stuck paying your dues," remember, on-the-job time is always learning time. You're constantly fine-tuning your technical chops, judgment and communication skills, and personal style, all of which are important building blocks in your career. Make the most of every situation.

The more time you spend familiarizing yourself with sound, whether in the studio, listening to live music, or working on location, the better equipped you'll be to develop your own "sonic personality," as legendary engineer Bruce Swedien discovered back when he was a fledgling engineer: "I was starting at Universal in Chicago and recording with Count Basie's band—this was in 1960 or 1962—and I was doing a straight-ahead album with Basie's band and Joe Williams, and we did a piece of music [called 'Night Time is the Right Time'] that started out with a trombone solo, and then Joe Williams sang a verse, and the next verse there was a trombone solo, and I desperately wanted to have my personality be a part of this incredible recording, so I said to the trombone player, 'When it comes time to play your solo, step up and tippie toe over to the corner of the room and play your solo into the corner of the room away from all the microphones, so that we'll hear only the reflected sound.' We were recording late at night or early in the morning, but one of the owners of the studio happened to come by—I think mainly to check up on me because I was kind of a kid. He saw what I was doing and was just livid. He was furious! He came to me and said, 'What are you doing? You can't do that! Music is never recorded with the musicians off-mic!' But everybody else loved it. It was an incredible thing, and it worked really well. What I accomplished was having my personality become a part of that recording. It really was effective, because the trombone solo comes from all around the room. I almost got my ass fired for that!"

In this career, you'll have to be a self-learner. If you step away and look back at your day-to-day experiences, you'll realize you've been doing that all along. But if you want to move ahead, you need to be proactive. Chances are, you've had to stay on top of technology out of necessity, since as the assistant engineer, you're most likely the one people turn to with technical problems, and you've probably learned that "I don't know" is the wrong answer. Conquer every piece of audio gear you can get your hands on. Read manuals, experiment. The more you know about equipment you already have, the easier it will be to figure out one more new piece of gear. Other ways to grow? Read the trades, cover to cover. Attend lectures and seminars, take night classes.

You can never have enough education, and broadening your skills broadens opportunities. In this cutthroat climate, you'll need to be as marketable as possible. Sure, you've got killer mixing chops, but what else can you offer? In today's global economy, you may be dealing with clients in other countries, from other cultures. Knowing a second language can give you a career edge over the competition. Pick up some extra maintenance skills; these days, more studios are outsourcing maintenance work to freelancers rather than keeping techs on staff, and if you offer great maintenance and troubleshooting skills in addition to mixing chops, you'll have more value to your employer. If you're really good at it, you could pick up some freelance maintenance work. If you're thinking of heading out on your own, take some business classes. Get fluent in general software applications. Look at your education as a continuing investment in your career.

MOVING ON

Sometimes, the only way to move up in your work is to leave the comfort of your existing job. There will be times when you take calculated career risks and they can really pay off. But make sure you examine these risks carefully. "I had a friend who moved to Denmark for two years for a great project and when he came back, people were like, 'Who are you?'" says Kevin Becka. The point is, you really have to weigh your options as far as how much income you need to make a living and how much you can afford to lose by making a jump and taking a leap of faith. Some engineers constantly move around, others work with the same artist for 20 years. It's up to you to determine the best opportunities for you.

It's important to keep your career timing in perspective. I know someone who rose from intern to assistant engineer to engineer very quickly, and then grew frustrated when she remained in the same position. She felt like her career was stalling, yet she was only 24 years old and had been the business a mere three years. If you were to ask the top engineers in this industry how long it took them get where they are today, you'd find it took them a lot longer than three years. And you have to remember that there are plenty of people leading successful careers in audio who never reach superstar status. "The path to success in audio is rarely linear," says Tufts's Paul Lehrman. "The stories you hear about fabulous engineers' and producers' lives on 'MTV Cribs' are not the norm—they are the tip of the iceberg. There's a lot more going on underneath the media's line of vision."

If you're thinking of moving on, you may find it's better to job hunt while you're still employed, so you won't feel pressure to find something right away before depleting your savings. On the other hand, job hunting can be full-time work, and if you've got the resources, it might be more ideal for you to dedicate all of your time and effort to the search.

If you do decide to leave your job, it's important to leave on good terms. Even if you're upset with your employer, as tempting as it may be to tell them all where to go, don't allow yourself to burn bridges. Be gracious and considerate—no drama scenes. You never know when you may need a reference, or if people will turn up somewhere else in your life in the future. Remember, this is a tiny industry and people talk. Save the venting for your friends.

Perhaps you're considering making the leap to freelance. There's a clear trend toward being self-employed in the audio industry, as least as far as the recording studio community goes. If you want to be your own boss, know the benefits, and the risks. "Freelancing is very hard on one's soul," says stage sound designer Janet Kalas, "because sometimes the layoff periods are very long and you feel like a failure. You feel like you're never going to work again and that's the end of your life, and then you get a job and it's the best show you've ever done and you can't quit. It's so bizarre."

If you aspire to go freelance, or even eventually run your own recording studio, you're going to need clientele. I talked about getting out on the local music scene and meeting artists and offering them free session time. This is important for networking, but crucial if you're trying to build up a client list.

FINDING YOUR NICHE

At this point in your career, you're getting into a groove: You know what aspects of your work excite you, and you're finally getting recognized for your talents. You may find yourself drawn into new areas of audio, opportunities to carve a career niche for yourself. It's time to take inventory of your interests and skills. Learn what sets you apart.

"Know your passion, what obsesses you," says Chris Pelonis, who evolved from studio engineering to designing studios and developing custom monitor designs. "For me, it's perfection; it's the ability to get purity in my listening environment, because I love music so much. I want to be able to hear the most true, accurate representation of whatever I record or someone else records, so there's no guessing and I can really get into the music. It's built a career for me. But the driving force is the factor.

"Some people, they're just wandering through this music world, and they may think, 'Hey, I really enjoy engineering, but guess what? I can really do some modifications to some of these microphones that would make them so much better,'" Pelonis continues. "You just find where your talents lie, and if you do something that other people get off on and helps other people, that's your first indication, that 'Wow, I'm really being appreciated. I'm really helping people by doing *a*, *b*, and *c*, and when I do *d* I'm kind of hitting a brick wall and it's not really working.' It's like a hit record: You can't force a record to be a hit, and when it's a hit you can't stop it."

Maybe you've discovered that you want to switch fields. Hardly any of us are doing what we thought we would be doing when we grew up. It's natural for your career to veer off path as your interests and skills develop over time. Although the technical skills required for many areas of audio are the same, the application is different. And don't overlook lifestyle factors. Say you want to make the switch from TV post to live sound. You'll face long stretches of work and periods of downtime. You might be used to working pretty consistent hours. How will you deal with the change? Make informed choices.

STRIVE FOR LIFE BALANCE

The thing that probably surprises new engineers the most is how much work their job is. You may be perfectly happy to do everything, but you might not realize how easily the work can take over other aspects of your life. "I think one of the most revealing moments for me was when I was on the educational board of directors for a school in Nashville and we had a lunch one time where we had all these top studio guys, and we were talking about audio and one guy said, 'I've gone through three marriages just because of this business,'" remembers CRAS' Kevin Becka. "If you're on a top level, you're really expected to work long, long hours and be there when a producer wants to work. And if he wants to work 1:00 pm to 3:00 am, that doesn't really lend itself to having a relationship with somebody." Don't be a martyr—take vacations! Nobody looks back at the end of their life and wishes they'd worked *more*. Workaholics, don't worry: Time away from work will refresh you, making you work more efficiently when you return.

As much as you may love your vocation, it's important to remember that your job is not your life. "You need to find a balance, and part of that balance might mean doing something in audio that will give you the balance you need in the rest of your life," says Kevin Becka. "It can really take over your life, and you might say, 'I worked with the Stones,' but ultimately, what does that mean?"

Make sure you always protect your greatest asset: Your ears. According to the House Ear Institute in Los Angeles, hearing loss is America's largest, yet least recognized, health ailment, affecting one out of every ten people. We are all exposed to varying levels of noise pollution as we go about our daily lives, and in the audio world, we can be subjected to extended periods of unhealthy, even dangerous decibel levels, especially in touring situations. Hearing health is crucial to success as an audio engineer, so make sure you understand the risks of prolonged exposure to high noise levels and learn how to reduce ear fatigue and protect your hearing. Nonprofit organizations such as the House Ear Institute and H.E.A.R. in San Francisco are dedicated to educating music professionals on hearing issues and promoting hearing health. Visit their Websites (see the Resources section in the back of this book) for resources on tinnitus, hearing loss, hearing evaluation referrals, and links to ear mold manufacturers (for ear plugs). Take your hearing health very seriously; hearing damage is irreversible.

Other health considerations? Audio engineers are subjected to long hours in awkward physical positions, slumped in bad chairs, and hunched over faders and knobs. Minimize the potential for carpal tunnel, back problems, and other physical ailments by working in an ergonomically sound environment. At the risk of sounding like your mom, sit up straight! Take an occasional walk around the block. At the very least, get up and stretch once in a while.

According to *Business Week*, there's a one in three chance we'll lose our jobs at least once in our lifetime. The odds are stacked even higher against you in the audio industry. So, be smart about money and have a long-term financial plan. Be ready in the event that you might have to be self-sustaining for a while. San Francisco engineer David Ogilvy shares his favorite strategy for getting through lean times: "I always recommend starting your own garden, so if you're really not working, you can still eat," he says with a laugh. "For about a year, about half the food I ate came out of my garden."

Finally, the best of us fall upon troubled times and it's good to know there are support groups out there to help. The National Academy of Recording Arts and Sciences' MusiCares Foundation was founded to provide confidential help for music professionals in times of financial, medical, or personal crisis. An emergency financial assistance program provides funds for medical bills and other expenses, and its addiction-recovery program provides referrals and financial assistance for the cost of addiction treatment. The foundation also organizes outreach events such as panels, health fairs, and workshops.

Giving Back to the Community

Now that you're becoming established in the industry, start thinking about acting as a role model to those coming up. It's a great way to give back to the community, while continuing your own learning. Stay in touch with your alma mater, get involved in association outreach programs, or seek out your own opportunities locally. Tufts University's Paul Lehrman stresses the importance of mentoring: "We're still a people-driven industry, and having someone to show you the way, especially by example, is incredibly helpful. And once you've found your way, it's only right—and highly useful—to turn back around and show the next generation how you did it."

"I think it's important to speak about the things that are unspoken, which are the business aspects, how you need to ensure that after say you go out and take that chance with these bands, how you would be paid and/or compensated," adds NARAS's Producers and Engineers wing director Leslie Lewis. "I think understanding how that works and understanding your value, and how to place that value in the marketplace, especially if you don't have the manager or lawyer or representative; veteran producers and engineers who are in it understand that. They've got great stories to tell, and you'll be able to learn from their mistakes."

As an audio engineer, you also have the means to give back to the larger community. "You've really got to support the arts," says designer Chris Pelonis. "To me, this is all about art. The fact that there's science involved to create the art, that's all great. But the performing arts, that's really where all change comes about." Pelonis shares an example of a project he recently began work on, a performing arts center on a Paiute Indian reservation in northern California. In addition to designing the facility, he's arranging guest visits from his high-profile musician friends. "The reason I really got excited about this project is because I want to see these kids have the same opportunities that the 'Hollywood nephews' have. They were always in the studio, surrounded by producers and great equipment. How about some poverty-stricken kids living in an Indian tribe in the desert having the same opportunity?" Pelonis says the center is also important for spreading cultural awareness. "It's important for our kids to be able to hear the musical expression and feelings and souls of kids that come from that culture," he says. "They've never had the opportunity to experience anything from these other kids. They're all just kids. And they should be able to share that."

A Long-Term Strategy For Success

If someone had told me 15 years ago, back when I was just starting music school, that I'd be writing and editing for a living, I would have laughed. There's no way to predict your career path, but most of the professionals I've met owe their success to taking a long-term strategic approach, using each career move as a stepping stone. Many have taken jobs along the way that may not have been the most desirable work, or the most gratifying, but they knew those jobs would open doors for them later on down the line. So that job you're considering that may not seem like the perfect gig right now may serve as the springboard to an ideal position later. Think long term.

"One of my professors said, 'What's important is to get on the train going the right way,'" says Dolby engineer Roy Jorge. "Your position might not be ideal at first, but once you get there you'll be learning a lot, and as long as you put yourself in a position that you can benefit from later on, that's important." Look at any time spent on a job as an investment: You're enhancing your skill set, building experiences, and developing a network of contacts for the rest of your career. So get your act together and put yourself in the path of success. Remain positive and keep an open mind. Lastly, remember that you grow day by day, and learning is a process that never ends. Good luck, and see you in the biz!

INDUSTRY FOUNDATIONS/ SUPPORT GROUPS

H.E.A.R.
Box 460847
San Francisco, CA 94115
(415) 409-3277
www.hearnet.com

House Ear Institute
2100 W. 3rd. St.
Los Angeles, CA 90057
(213) 483-4431
www.hei.org

Mix Foundation for Excellence in Audio
1547 Palos Verdes Mall, #294
Walnut Creek, CA 94596
(925) 939-6149
www.tecawards.org

MusiCares Foundation
West Coast:
3402 Pico Boulevard
Santa Monica, CA 90405
(310) 392-3777
Toll-free helpline: (800) 687-4227

Central:
1904 Wedgewood Avenue
Nashville, TN 37212
(615) 327-0050
Toll-free helpline: (877) 626-2748

Northeast:
156 West 56th Street, Suite 1701
New York, NY 10019
(212) 245-7840
Toll-free helpline: (877) 303-6962
www.grammy.com/musicares/index.aspx

Women's Audio Mission
P.O. Box 410663
San Francisco, CA 94141
(415) 425-1597
www.womensaudiomission.com

AUDIO INDUSTRY ORGANIZATIONS

Academy of Television Arts & Sciences
5220 Lankershim Blvd.
North Hollywood, CA 91601
(818) 754-2800
www.emmys.tv

American Electronics Association
5201 Great America Parkway, Suite 520
Santa Clara, CA 95054
(408) 987-4200
www.aeanet.org

American Federation of Musicians
1501 Broadway, Suite 600
New York, NY 10036
(212) 869-1330
www.afm.org

American Federation of TV & Radio Artists
New York office:
260 Madison Avenue
New York, NY 10016
(212) 532-0800

Los Angeles office:
5757 Wilshire Blvd., 9th Floor
Los Angeles, CA 90036
(323) 634-8100
www.aftra.com

American Women in Radio & Television, Inc.
1595 Spring Hill Road, Suite 330
Vienna, VA 22182
(703) 506-3290
www.awrt.org

Audio Engineering Society
60 East 42nd Street, Suite 2520
New York, NY 10165
(212) 661-8528
www.aes.org

Canadian Academy of Recording Arts & Sciences
124 Merton Street, Suite 305
Toronto, ON M4S 2Z2
Canada
(416) 485-3135
www.juno-awards.ca

Canadian Recording Industry Association
890 Yonge Street, Suite 1200
Toronto, ON M4W 3P4
Canada
(416) 967-7272
www.cria.ca

The Cinema Audio Society
12414 Huston Street
Valley Village, CA 91607
(818) 752-8624
www.cinemaaudiosociety.org

Game Audio Network Guild
P.O. Box 1001
San Juan Capistrano, CA 92393
www.audiogang.org

International Radio & Television Society
420 Lexington Avenue, Suite 1601
New York, NY 10170
(212) 867-6650
www.irts.org

Latin Academy of Recording Arts & Sciences
311 Lincoln Road, Suite 301
Miami, FL 33139
(305) 672-0047
www.grammy.com/latin-academy

Los Angeles Music Network
P.O. Box 8934
Universal City, CA 91618-8934
(818) 769-6095
www.lamn.com

Motion Picture Sound Editors
10061 Riverside Dr.
PMB No. 751
Toluca Lake, CA 91602
(818) 506-7731
www.mpse.org

Nashville Association of Professional Recording Services
P.O. Box 128511
Nashville, TN 37212
www.naprs.org

National Academy of Recording Arts & Sciences
3402 Pico Blvd.
Santa Monica, CA 90405
(310) 392-3777
www.grammy.com

National Association of Broadcasters
1771 "N" Street NW
Washington, DC 20036
(202) 429-5300
www.nab.org

National Association of Record Industry Professionals
P.O. Box 8934
Universal City, CA 91618
(818) 769-7007
www.narip.com

National Systems Contracting Association
625 First Street SE, Suite 420
Cedar Rapids, IA 52401
(800) 446-NSCA
www.nsca.org

Recording Industry Association of America
1330 Connecticut Avenue NW, Suite 300
Washington, DC 20036
(202) 775-0101
www.riaa.com

Recording Musicians Association
817 Vine Street, Suite 209
Hollywood, CA 90038
(323) 462-4762
www.rmaweb.org

Society of Motion Picture & Television Engineers
595 West Hartsdale Avenue
White Plains, NY 10607
(914) 761-1100
www.smpte.org

Society of Professional Audio Recording Services
9 Music Sq. S., Suite 222
Nashville, TN 37203
(800) 771-7727
www.spars.com

Washington Area Music Association
1101 17th Street NW, Suite 1100
Washington, DC 20036
(202) 338-1134
www.wamadc.com

Women in Music National Network
31121 Mission Blvd., Suite 300
Hayward, CA 94544-7603
(510) 232-3897
www.womeninmusic.com

AUDIO EDUCATION PROGRAMS

The Academy of Production & Recording Arts
619 11th Ave. SE
Calgary, Alberta T2G 0Y8
Canada
(403) 237-8561
www.apra.ca
Degrees/certificates offered: Sound Basics 101 certificate; Music Advanced certificate; Post-Production Advanced

Alexander Magazine
14071 Stephens
Suite #A-5
Warren, MI 48089
(877) 683-1743
www.alexandermagazine.com
Degrees/certificates offered: Recording Techniques 1 and Associate Recording Engineer programs.

Alta Center for Communication Arts
9014 N. 23rd Ave., Suite 1
Phoenix, AZ 85021
(888) 729-4954
www.thealtacenter.com
Degrees/certificates offered: Diploma in 10-week Digital Audio Recording program

American University
4400 Massachusetts Ave. N.W.
Washington, DC 20016-8058
(202) 885-2746
www.american.edu
Degrees/certificates offered: Bachelor of Science in Audio Technology, Minor in Audio Technology

Appalachian State University
Hayes School of Music
Boone, NC 28608
(828) 262-3020
www.music.appstate.edu/recording
Degrees/certificates offered: Bachelor of Science in Music Industry Studies. Also, Bachelor of Music in Performance, Education, and Music Therapy

Art Institute of Seattle
2323 Elliott Ave.
Seattle, WA 98103
(206) 239-2338
www.ais.edu
Degrees/certificates offered: Six-quarter AA in Audio Production

Aspen Music Festival and School
2 Music School Rd.
Aspen, CO 81611
(970) 925-3254
www.aspenmusicfestival.com
Degrees/certificates offered: The Edgar Stanton Audio Recording Institute four-week, full-time seminar/workshop

Audio Engineering Institute
6610 Buffalo Hills
San Antonio, TX 78256-2330
(210) 698-9666
www.audio-eng.com
Degrees/certificates offered: Basic and advanced Audio Engineering classes, each lasting 10 weeks

Audio Institute of America
P.O. Box 15427
San Francisco, CA 94115
(415) 752-0701
www.audioinstitute.com
Degrees/certificates offered: Home-study diploma in recording engineering

Audio Recording Technology Institute, New York
100-4, 5 Patco Ct.
Islandia, NY 11749
(631) 582-8999
www.audiotraining.com
Degrees/certificates offered: Certificate offered for graduates of eight-month program

Audio Recording Technology Institute, Florida
4525 Vineland Rd. Suite 201
Orlando, FL 32811
(888) 543-2784
www.audiocareer.com
Degrees/certificates offered: 45-week Audio Engineering certificate

The Banff Centre
107 Tunnel Mountain Dr.
Box 1020
Banff, Alberta T1L 1H5
Canada
(403) 762-6180
www.BanffCentre.ca
Degrees/certificates offered: One- to six-term Audio Assistant and Associate Work/Study programs

Barton College
Box 5000
Wilson, NC 27893
(800) 345-4973
www.barton.edu
Degrees/certificates offered: Bachelor of Arts in Mass Communication, Audio Recording Technology Concentration

Belmont University
Mike Curb College of Entertainment and Music Business
1900 Belmont Blvd.
Nashville, TN 37212-3757
(615) 460-5504
www.belmont.edu
Degrees/certificates offered: Bachelor of Business Administration with emphasis in Music Business

Berklee College of Music
1140 Boylston St.
Boston, MA 02215
(800) BERKLEE
www.berklee.edu
Degrees/certificates offered: Bachelor of Music or four-year Professional Diploma

Berkleemusic.com
Online branch of Berklee college of Music
www.berkleemusic.com
Degrees/certificates offered: Continuing Education Units, Certificates of Completion for instructor-led online courses

Butler University
4600 Sunset Ave.
Indianapolis, IN 46208
(317) 940-9828
www.butler.edu/mediaarts
Degrees/certificates offered: Bachelor of Science in Telecommunication Arts. Concentrations in Recording Industry Studies, Multimedia, Video Production, and Electronic Journalism

California State University, Chico
Department of Music
Chico, CA 95929-0805
(530) 898-5500
www.csuchico.edu/mus/
Degrees/certificates offered: Four-year Bachelor of Arts in Music with an option in Recording Arts; Bachelor of Arts in Music with an option in Music Industry

California State University, Dominguez Hills
1000 E. Victoria St.
Carson, CA 90247
(310) 243-3543
www.csudh.edu
Degrees/certificates offered: Four-year Bachelor of Arts in Audio Recording; Bachelor of Arts Music Technology; certificate in Audio Technology

Case Western Reserve University
Department of Music
Cleveland, OH 44106
(800) 808-MUSC
http://music.cwru.edu
Degrees/certificates offered: Four-year Bachelor of Arts in Audio Recording Technology, Five-year double major with electrical engineering

Central Carolina Community College
1105 Kelly Dr.
Sanford, NC 27330
(919) 718-7257
www.cccc.edu
Degrees/certificates offered: One-year diploma in Radio Production, one-year diploma in Television Production, two-year Associate Degree in Applied Science in Broadcast Production Technology

Central Missouri State University
CMSU Dept. of Music
Hudson 108
Warrensburg, MO 64093
(660) 543-4589
www.cmsu.edu/music/musictech/mutechindex.htm
Degrees/certificates offered: Bachelor of Music in Music Technology

Citrus College
1000 W Foothill Blvd.
Glendora, CA 91741
(626) 852-8061
www.citrusstudios.org
Degrees/certificates offered: One-year Vocation Certificate in Recording Technology

City College of New York
The Sonic Arts Center
Shepard Hall Room #72
West 140th and Convent Ave.
New York, NY 10031
(212) 650-8288
http://sonic.arts.ccny.cuny.edu/
Degrees/certificates offered: Bachelor of Fine Arts in Music, Audio Technology
concentration

City College of San Francisco
Broadcast Electronic Media Arts Department
50 Phelan St., Box A6
San Francisco, CA 94112
(415) 239-3527
www.ccsf.edu/Departments/Broadcast/
Degrees/certificates offered: Sound Recording Certificate and Sound Design Certificate

The Cleveland Institute of Music
11021 East Blvd.
Cleveland, OH 44106
(216) 791-5000
www.cim.edu
Degrees/certificates offered: Bachelor of Music in Audio Recording; double major
with an instrument or Composition major in five years

Cogswell Polytechnical College
1175 Bordeaux Drive
Sunnyvale, CA 94089
(408) 541-0100
www.cogswell.edu
Degrees/certificates offered: Bachelor of Science in Digital Audio Technology; Bachelor
of Science in Audio Engineering

The College of Saint Rose
432 Western Avenue
Albany, NY 12203
(518) 454-5178
www.strose.edu
Degrees/certificates offered: Bachelor of Science in Music, Music Industry Emphasis;
part-time Master of Arts in Music Technology

Collin County Community College
2800 E. Spring Creek Parkway
Plano, TX 75074
(972) 516-5041
www.ccccd.edu
Degrees/certificates offered: Two-year AAS in Commercial Music; one-year Certificate in Audio Engineering

Columbia Academy
1295 West Broadway
Vancouver, BC V6H 3X8
Canada
(604) 736-3316 or (800) 665-9283
www.columbia-academy.com
Degrees/certificates offered: One-year Diploma in Digital/Analog Recording Arts

Columbia College Chicago
Department of Audio Arts & Acoustics
600 South Michigan Ave.
Chicago, IL 60605
(312) 344-8800
www.colum.edu
Degrees/certificates offered: Bachelor of Arts in Audio Arts and Acoustics with concentrations in Music Recording, Concert Sound Reinforcement, Acoustics, Sound Contracting, and Sound for Picture

Conservatory of Recording Arts & Sciences
2300 East Broadway Rd.
Tempe, AZ 85282-1707
(800) 562-6383
www.audiorecordingschool.com
Degrees/certificates offered: 900-hour full-time Master Recording Program II program

Cuyahoga Community College
2900 Community College Ave.
Cleveland, OH 44115
(216) 987-4252
www.tri-c.edu/rat
Degrees/certificates offered: Two-year (five-semester) Associate of Applied Science degree in Recording Arts & Technology. Certified Pro Tools training center

Dallas Sound Lab
School for the Recording Arts
350 E. Royal Lane
Building 4, Suite 119
Irving, TX 75039
(866) 498-1122
www.dallassoundlab.com
Degrees/certificates offered: Diploma program in Audio Engineering and Studio Techniques; seminars in Music Business Administration, Audio Engineering for Film and Television Production, and Contemporary Music Theory

Del Mar College/Radio & Television
Baldwin & Ayers
Corpus Christi, TX 78404
(361) 698-1508
www.delmar.edu/comm/rtv/RTVHome1.html
Degrees/certificates offered: Radio & Television, two-year A.A. degree

DePaul University School of Music
804 W. Belden Ave.
Chicago, IL 60614
(773) 325-7444
music.depaul.edu
Degrees/certificates offered: Bachelor of Science degree in Music

Elmhurst College
190 Prospect
Elmhurst, IL 60126
(630) 617-3500
www.elmhurst.edu
Degrees/certificates offered: Bachelor of Music in Music Business, Bachelor of Science in Music Business, Bachelor of Music in Music Education, Bachelor of Arts in Music

Ex'pression College for Digital Arts
6601 Shellmound St.
Emeryville, CA 94608
(877) 833-8800
www.expression.edu
Degrees/certificates offered: Two-and-a-half year accelerated Bachelor degree in Sound Arts.
Degrees also offered in animation and graphic design

Fanshawe College
1460 Oxford St. East
London, Ontario N5Y 5RX
(519) 452-4130
www.fanshawec.ca
Degrees/certificates offered: Two-year Diploma in Music Industry Arts. One-year Post-Diploma Program in Digital Applications (Advanced Digital Audio and Digital Video Editing)

Finger Lakes Community College
4355 Lakeshore Dr.
Canandaigua, NY 14424
(585) 394-3500
www.fingerlakes.edu
Degrees/certificates offered: Two-year A.S. Music Recording Technology degree

Fits & Starts Productions, LLC
48 Riverdale Ave. East
Tinton Falls, NJ 07724
(732) 741-1275
www.modernrecording.com
Degrees/certificates offered: None—touring audio seminars

Five Towns College
305 North Service Rd.
Dix Hills, NY 11746
(631) 424-7000
www.fivetowns.edu
Degrees/certificates offered: Bachelor of Music in Jazz/Commercial Music, with concentrations in performance, composition/songwriting, musical theater, audio recording technology, music business and video music. Bachelor degree program in Music Education. Bachelor of Professional Studies (B.P.S.) Degree program in Business Management, with concentrations in audio recording technology, music business, video arts, and theater arts

Fred N. Thomas Career Education Center
2650 Eliot St.
Denver, CO 80211
(303) 964-3075
www.dosomethingreal.com/
Degrees/certificates offered: Public high-school program

Full Sail Real World Education
3300 University Blvd.
Winter Park, FL 32792
(800) 226-7625
www.fullsail.com
Degrees/certificates offered: Associate of Science Degrees in Computer Animation, Digital Media, Film, Game Design & Development, Recording Arts, and Show Production & Touring. All degrees take 12-14 months to complete

Fullerton College
321 E. Chapman Ave.
Fullerton, CA 92832
(714) 992-7302
www.fullcoll.edu
Degrees/certificates offered: Music Production Recording Certificate as part of a Commercial Music major

Future Media Concepts
305 East 47th Street, Level C
New York, NY 10017
(212) 888-6314
www.FMCtraining.com
Degrees/certificates offered: Digidesign-authorized Pro Tools certification courses for "Operator" Music and/or Post Production; "Expert" Music and/or Post Production

Guilford Technical Community College
P.O. Box 309
601 High Point Rd.
Jamestown, NC 27282
(336) 334-4822
www.gtcc.edu
Degrees/certificates offered: Two-year A.A.S. in Entertainment Technology-Sound Engineering, Two-year A.A.S. in Entertainment Technology/Concert Sound & Lighting, Two-year A.A.S. in Entertainment Technology/Management, Two-year A.A.S. in Entertainment Technology/Performance, various subject-specific certificates and one-year diplomas

Globe Institute of Recording and Production
P.O. Box 961
Brisbane, CA 94005
(800) 9000-MIX
www.GlobeRecording.com
Degrees/certificates offered: Two-year Audio Producer Associate Degree; four-month certificates in Audio Recording and Production, Music Business, Digital Composition, Audio for Media, Digital Audio Workstation (Pro Tools), and PsychoAcoustics—Sound Healing

Golden West College
15744 Goldenwest St.
Huntington Beach, CA 92647
(714) 895-8780
www.gwc.info
Degrees/certificates offered: Commercial Musician/Recording Arts certificate

Grand Valley State University
1 Campus Dr.
Allendale, MI 49401
(800) 748-0246
www.gvsu.edu
Degrees/certificates offered: Electrical Engineering with Music minor

Hampton University
Department of Music
Hampton, VA 23668
(757) 727-5237
www.hamptonu.edu
Degrees/certificates offered: Bachelor of Science in Music with an emphasis in music engineering technology

Harris Institute for the Arts
118 Sherbourne St.
Toronto, Ontario M5A 2R2
Canada
(416) 367-0178
www.harrisinstitute.com
Degrees/certificates offered: One-year diploma. Programs in Recording Arts Management (RAM) and Producing/Engineering Program (PEP)

Houston Community College
1010 W. Sam Houston Parkway N.
Houston, TX 77043
(713) 718-5621
http://nwc.hccs.edu/av
Degrees/certificates offered: Two-year AAS degrees in Audio Recording or Film Production. One-year certificates in Audio Recording, MIDI, Film Production, Film Editing, or Scriptwriting

Howard University
Dept. of Radio, TV, & Film
525 Bryant Street N.W., Rm. 230
Washington, DC 20059
(202) 806-7927
www.howard.edu
Degrees/certificates offered: Bachelor of Arts in audio production; Bachelor of Arts in Television Production; Bachelor of Arts in Film Production; Bachelor of Arts in Telecommunications Management; two-year MFA in Film

Indiana University
School of Music
Bloomington, IN 47405
(812) 855-1087
www.music.indiana.edu/som/audio
Degrees/certificates offered: Associate of Science in Audio Technology, Bachelor of Science in Recording Arts

Institute of Audio Research
64 University Place
New York, NY 10003
(212) 777-8550
www.audioschool.com
Degrees/certificates offered: Diploma in Audio Recording and Production, Bachelor Degree credit at participating universities and colleges

Ithaca College School of Music
3322 Whalen Center for Music
Ithaca, NY 14850
(607) 274-3366
www.ithaca.edu/music
Degrees/certificates offered: Bachelor of Music in Sound Recording Technology

International College of Broadcasting
6 So. Smithville Rd.
Dayton, OH 45431
(937) 258-8251
www.icbproductions.com
Degrees/certificates offered: Associate Degree program in Applied Science of Communication Arts in Television and Radio, Associate Degree program of Applied Science in Video Production/Recording, Audio Engineer Diploma program in Recording Audio Engineering, Diploma program in Broadcasting

Kansas City Kansas Community College
7250 State Ave.
Kansas City, KS 66112
(913) 288-7634
www.kckcc.edu/music
Degrees/certificates offered: Associate of Applied Science Degree in Audio Engineering; Associate of General Studies Degree in Music Technology

Labette Community College
200 S. 14th
Parsons, KS 67357
(888) LABETTE ext.1020
www.labette.edu/commusic/home.htm
Degrees/certificates offered: A.A.S. in Commercial Music Performance; A.A.S. in Commercial Music Technology

Lakeland Community College
7700 Clocktower Dr.
Kirtland, OH 44094
(800) 589-8520
www.Lakelandcc.edu
Degrees/certificates offered: Two-year Certificates in Audio Engineering and Production, Video Production and Broadcast, Radio Engineering and Broadcast, Interactive Media Technology, Animation and Cartoon Arts, Interactive Entertainment Technology. Bachelor of Communications (with emphasis in above fields) through association with Notre Dame College

Lebanon Valley College of Pennsylvania
Department of Music
Annville, PA 17003
(717) 867-6275
www.lvc.edu/music
Degrees/certificates offered: Bachelor of Music in Music Recording Technology, Bachelor of Science in Music Business

Long Beach City College
4901 East Carson St.
Long Beach, CA 90808
(562) 938-4309
www.lbcc.cc.ca.us
Degrees/certificates offered: A.A. with emphasis in Commercial Music, 10 certificates in Music, Radio or Television

Los Angeles Recording Workshop
Center for the Recording Arts
5278 Lankershim Blvd.
North Hollywood, CA 91601
(818) 763-7400
www.recordingcareer.com
Degrees/certificates offered: 900-hour Recording Engineer Certificate Program

Los Medanos College
2700 E. Leland Rd.
Pittsburg, CA 94565
(925) 439-0200
www.losmedanos.edu
Degrees/certificates offered: Two-year AA in Recording Arts and two-year Recording Arts Certificate

Loyola Marymount University
One LMU Drive
MS-8230
Los Angeles, CA 90045
(310) 338-4575
www.lmu.edu
Degrees/certificates offered: Bachelor of Arts in Recording Arts (music recording and film sound)

Madison Media Institute
2102 Agriculture Dr.
Madison, WI 53718
(608) 663-2000
www.madisonmedia.com
Degrees/certificates offered: Associate of Arts in Recording and Music Technology, Associate of Arts in Multimedia Technology, Video Production diploma

McGill University
Faculty of Music
555 Sherbrooke St. West
Montreal, Quebec H3A 1E3
Canada
(514) 398-4535
www.music.mcgill.ca/mmt
Degrees/certificates offered: Master of Music Degree in Sound Recording; Ph.D. Degree

Mediatech Institute
6305 N. O'Connor Blvd.
Irving, TX 75039
(866) 498-1122
www.mediatechinstitute.com
Degrees/certificates offered: Diploma/certification programs in Audio Engineering and Studio Techniques, Producing & Songwriting, Music Business Administration, TV & Film Soundtrack Production, Live Sound Reinforcement, and Multimedia Production

Mercy College Center for Digital Arts
277 Martine Ave.
White Plains, NY 10601
(914) 948-3666
www.mercy.edu/cda
Degrees/certificates offered: Bachelor of Science in Music Industry and Technology

Mesa Community College
1835 West Southern Ave.
Mesa, AZ 85202
(480) 461-7273
www.mc.maricopa.edu
Degrees/certificates offered: Associate of Applied Science Degree in Music Technology: Studio Recording, approximately two years; or Certificate of Completion (CCL), approximately one year

Miami-Dade Community College
School of Film and Video
11380 N.W. 27th Ave.
Miami, FL 33167
(305) 237-1185
www.mdcc.edu/dfvbeta
Degrees/certificates offered: Associate Science Degree in Radio, Television, Broadcast Programming; Associate Science Degree in Film Production; Certificate in Television Production; Associate Arts Degree in Mass Communication

Middle Tennessee State University
P.O. Box 21
Murfreesboro, TN 37132
(615) 898-2578
www.mtsu.edu/~record
Degrees/certificates offered: Bachelor of Science in Recording Industry

Mills College
5000 MacArthur Blvd.
Oakland, CA 94613
(510) 430-2191
Degrees/certificates offered: Bachelor of Arts specializing in composition with an emphasis on technology. Master of Fine Arts degrees in composition can specialize in electronic music and recording media. Mills is an undergraduate women's college and a co-educational graduate college.

Minneapolis Community & Technical College
1501 Hennepin Ave.
Minneapolis, MN 55403
(612) 659-6000
www.minneapolis.edu
Degrees/certificates offered: Two-year A.S. in Sound Arts

Minnesota State University, Moorhead
1104 7th Ave. S.
Moorhead, MN 56563
(218) 477-2101
www.mnstate.edu/music
Degrees/certificates offered: Bachelor of Music, Music Industry; Master of Music, New Media (flexible program)

MiraCosta College
Music Department
1 Barnard Dr.
Oceanside, CA 92056
(760) 757-2121 x6703
www.miracosta.edu/music
Degrees/certificates offered: A.A. in Music. Certificates in Recording Arts/Record Production, Computerized Audio Production, Sound Reinforcement, Music Technology, and Performance Technician

Mt. San Jacinto College
1499 North State St.
San Jacinto, CA 92583
(909) 487-6752 x1577
www.msjc.edu
Degrees/certificates offered: Audio Technologies Certificate (18 units), Associate Degree, Audio Technologies

Musictech College
19 Exchange St. East
Saint Paul, MN 55101
(800) 594-9500
www.musictech.edu
Degrees/certificates offered: Two-year Associate of Applied Science (AAS) degrees; one-year Diploma programs; four-year Bachelor degrees offered through a direct-transfer agreement with Augsburg College

Musitechnic Educational Services Inc.
888, de Maisonneuve East
Tower 3, Suite 440
Montreal, Quebec H2L 4S8
Canada
www.musitechnic.com
Degrees/certificates offered: Computer Assisted Sound Design, one year; Attestation of Collegial Studies (A.E.C.)

Nassau Community College
One Education Dr.
Garden City, NY 11530
(516) 572-7446
www.sunynassau.edu
Degrees/certificates offered: One-year certificate in Studio Recording Technology

The New England Institute of Art
10 Brookline Place West
Brookline, MA 02445-7295
(800) 903-4425
www.neia.aii.edu
Degrees/certificates offered: Two-year Associate of Science in Audio Production; four-year Bachelor of Science in Audio & Media Technology

New England School of Communications
1 College Circle
Bangor, ME 04401
(888) 877-1876
www.nescom.edu
Degrees/certificates offered: Two-year Associate of Science in Communications, Audio Engineering Concentration; Four-year Bachelor of Science in Communications, Audio Engineering Concentration

New York University
School of Education
Department of Music and Performing Arts Professions
35 West 4th St., Room 777
New York, NY 10012-1172
(212) 998-5422
www.education.nyu.edu/music
Degrees/certificates offered: Bachelor of Arts in Recording Arts; two-year certificate in Music Business; Bachelor of Music; Master of Music in Music Technology

Northeast Community College
801 East Benjamin Ave.
Norfolk, NE 68701
(402) 844-7365
www.northeastaudio.org
Degrees/certificates offered: Two-year AAS in Audio/Recording Technology

Northeastern University
Department of Music
351 Ryder Hall
Boston, MA 02115
(617) 373-2400
www.music.neu.edu/
Degrees/certificates offered: Bachelor of Science in Music Industry; Bachelor of Science in Music Technology (Composition for New Media); Bachelor of Arts in Music Literature and Performance; and Bachelor of Science dual major in Multimedia Studies and Music Technology

NY Institute for Forensic Audio
P.O. Box 189
Colonia, NJ 07067
(732) 574-9672
www.owlinvestigations.com
Degrees/certificates offered: Video Authenticity certification, Audio Authenticity certification, Voice Identification

NYC College of Technology/Entertainment Technology
300 Jay St. #V411
Brooklyn, NY 11201
(718) 260-5588
www.citytech.cuny.edu/academics/deptsites/enttech/indexs.html
Degrees/certificates offered: BT in entertainment technology. Certificates in sound, lighting, scenic construction, and show control technologies

NYU Steinhart School
35 West 4th St.
Suite 777
New York, NY 10012
(212) 998-5422
www.nyu.edu/education/music/mtech/
Degrees/certificates offered: Bachelor of Music in Music Technology; Master of Music in Music Technology, Scoring for Film and Multimedia Sequence; Master of Music in Music Technology Tonemeister Honors Sequence that includes Tonemeister Certification

Oberlin Conservatory of Music
TIMARA Department
Oberlin, OH 44074
(440) 775-8413
www.timara.oberlin.edu
Degrees/certificates offered: Bachelor of Music, Bachelor of Arts in Visual Arts with an emphasis in Digital Media

Ocean County Vocational Technical Schools
Audio Recording for Electronic Media Career & Technical Institute
P.O. Box 1125, NAVAIR
Lakehurst, NJ 08733-1125
(732) 657-4000
www.ocvts.org
Degrees/certificates offered: One- and two-year Audio Engineering certificates offered to high school and post-secondary students

Ohio University, School of Telecommunications
9 S. College St.
Athens, OH 45701
(740) 593-4870
www.tcomschool.ohio.edu
Degrees/certificates offered: Bachelor of Science in Communications with one of three tracks in audio production: Music Recording, Media Production, or Audio Post-Production for Moving Image

Oklahoma State University-Stillwater
Department of Music
Stillwater, OK 74078
(405) 744-6133
www.osu.okstate.edu
Degrees/certificates offered: Bachelor of Music in Music Business, Music Education, Music Performance; Bachelor of Arts, and Master of Music in Pedagogy and Performance. Courses in Music Technology and Recording Techniques

Omega Recording Studios
School of Applied Recording Arts and Sciences
5609 Fishers Lane
Rockville, MD 20852
(301) 230-9100
www.omegastudios.com
Degrees/certificates offered: Five certificate programs; an Avid-authorized education center

Ontario Institute of Audio Recording Technology
502 Newbold St.
London, Ontario, N6E 1K6
Canada
(519) 686-5010
www.oiart.ca
Degrees/certificates offered: One-year diploma in Audio Recording Technology

Pacific Audio Visual Institute
34 West 8th Avenue
Vancouver, BC V5Y 1M7
Canada
(604) 873-4853
www.pacificav.com
Degrees/certificates offered: One-year Audio Engineering and Production diploma; one-year Film & Music Business diploma; one-year Indie Filmmaker diploma

Parsons Center for Audio Studies
192 Worcester St.
Wellesley, MA 02481
(781) 431-8708 x11
www.paudio.com
Degrees/certificates offered: Certificate of Completion

Peabody Institute of Johns Hopkins University
1 East Mount Vernon Place
Baltimore, MD 21202
(410) 659-8100 x8136
www.peabody.jhu.edu/recording-arts
Degrees/certificates offered: Five-year Bachelor Degree in Recording Arts, two-year Master's degree in Audio Recording and Acoustics

Penn State University
103 Arts Building
University Park, PA 16802
(814) 863-4879
www.psu.edu
Degrees/certificates offered: BFA in Technical Theatre (Sound Design); Bachelor of Arts in Integrative Arts

Pro Tools Training Center, Miami
1926 NE 154th Street
North Miami Beach, FL 33162
(888) 277-0457
www.protoolstraining.com
Degrees/certificates offered: Digidesign Pro Tools Operator Certification-Music or Post-Production, Digidesign Pro Tools Expert Certification-Music or Post-Production

Pyramind
880 Folsom St.
San Francisco, CA 94107
(415) 896-9800
www.pyramind.com
Degrees/certificates offered: Producer, Composer, and Film Audio Certificate Programs. Digidesign Pro Tools Certified Training, Apple Logic Audio Certified Training

Recording Arts Canada
P.O. Box 11025
984 Hwy #8
Stoney Creek, Ontario L8E 5P9
Canada
(888) 662-2664 or (905) 662-2666
www.recordingarts.com
Degrees/certificates offered: Diploma in audio engineering and multimedia production

Recording Institute of Detroit
14611 9-Mile Rd.
Eastpointe, MI 48021
(800) 683-1743
http://recordinginstitute.com
Degrees/certificates offered: Recording Engineer Certificate; Music Producer Certificate; Associate Recording Engineer Certificate

The Recording Workshop
455 Massieville Rd.
Chillicothe, OH 45601
(800) 848-9900
www.recordingworkshop.com
Degrees/certificates offered: Certificates in Recording Engineering and Music Production, Studio Maintenance and Troubleshooting, Advanced Recording Engineering and Music Production, NewTech Computer-Based Audio Production

Ridgewater College
Audio Technology Program
2 Century Ave.
Hutchinson, MN 55350
(800) 222-4424
www.ridgewater.mnscu.edu
Degrees/certificates offered: Two-year diploma in Audio Technology, two-year A.A.S. Degree in Audio Technology

Rose State College
6420 S.E. 15th St.
Midwest City, OK 73110
(405) 733-7426
www.rose.edu/faculty/cwhite
Degrees/certificates offered: Two-year Liberal Studies Degree with Music Recording option

SAE Institute of Technology
1293 Broadway, 9th floor
New York, NY 10001
(212) 944-9121
www.sae.edu
Degrees/certificates offered: Nine-month/18-month Audio Technology Diploma (full time/part time), nine-month Multimedia Producer Diploma (full time)

San Diego City College
1313 Park Blvd.
San Diego, CA 92101
(619) 388-3337
www.city.sdccd.cc.ca.us
Degrees/certificates offered: Two-year A.A. Degree in Electronic Music

San Francisco State University
1600 Holloway Ave.
San Francisco, CA 94132
(415) 338-1787
www.sfsu.edu
Degrees/certificates offered: Bachelor of Arts and Master of Arts in Radio and Television, with emphasis in music recording, audio-for-visual media, and audio post-production

Select Sound Studios
2315 Elmwood Ave.
Kenmore, NY 14217
(716) 873-2717
www.selectsound.com
Degrees/certificates offered: Six Recording Technologies programs; Each program is 12 weeks and three credits

Sheffield Institute for the Recording Arts
13816 Sunnybrook Rd.
Phoenix, MD 21131
(410) 628-7260
www.sheffieldav.com
Degrees/certificates offered: Certificate. AudioWorks Program: 290 clock hours/ full- or part-time Audio Engineering program. VideoWorks Program: 244 clock hours/full- or part-time Video Production program. TechWorks Program: 380 clock hours/full- or part-time Systems Integration, Installation, and Maintenance program

Shenandoah University
1460 University Dr.
Winchester, VA 22601
(540) 665-5567
www.su.edu
Degrees/certificates offered: Bachelor of Music, Commercial Music emphasis

Sound Master Recording Engineer School Audio/Video Institute
10747 Magnolia Blvd.
North Hollywood, CA 91601
(323) 650-8000
Degrees/certificates offered: Recording Engineering Certificate

South Plains College
Sound Technology Program
1401 S. College Ave.
Levelland, TX 79336
(806) 894-9611 x2276
www.southplainscollege.edu/creativearts/soundtechnology
Degrees/certificates offered: Two-year A.A.S. in Sound Technology

Southwest Texas State University
601 University Dr.
San Marcos, TX 78666
(512) 245-8451
www.swt.edu/music/srt/
Degrees/certificates offered: Bachelor of Music in Sound Recording Technology

Stanford CCRMA (Center for Computer Research in Music and Acoustics)
Department of Music
Stanford University
Stanford, CA 94305
(650) 723-4971
www-ccrma.stanford.edu
Degrees/certificates offered: Graduate interdisciplinary program

State University of New York College at Fredonia
1146 Mason Hall
Fredonia, NY 14063
(716) 673-4634
www.fredonia.edu/som/srt
Degrees/certificates offered: Bachelor of Science in Sound Recording Technology

Synergetic Audio Concepts Inc.
8780 Rufing Rd.
Greenville, IN 47124
(812) 923-0174
www.synaudcon.com
Degrees/certificates offered: Syn-Aud-Con "Week of Audio Training" includes System and Optimization and System Design

Texas State University
School of Music
601 University Drive
San Marcos, TX 78666
(512) 245-8451
www.txstate.edu/music/srt/
Degrees/certificates offered: Bachelor of Music in Sound Recording Technology

Trebas Institute, British Columbia
112 East 3rd Ave.
Vancouver, BC V5T 1C8
Canada
(604) 872-2666
www.trebas.com
Degrees/certificates offered: One-year diploma programs in Audio Engineering, Recorded Music Production, Music Business Administration, Film/Television Production and Film/Television Post-Production; Bachelor of Arts in Sound Technology in partnership with the Liverpool Institute for Performing Arts; and Bachelor of Arts in Enterprise Management

Trebas Institute, Ontario
149 College St.
Toronto, Ontario M5T 1P5
Canada
(416) 966-3066
www.trebas.com
Degrees/certificates offered: One-year diploma programs in Audio Engineering, Recorded Music Production, Music Business Administration, Film/Television Production, New-Media Development and 3-D Animation. Bachelor of Arts Degree in Sound Technology (two years, following one-year diploma in Audio Engineering) in partnership with the Liverpool Institute for Performing Arts

Trod Nossel Recording Studio
10 George St.
Wallingford, CT 06492
(203) 269-4465; (800) 800-HITS
www.trodnossel.com
Degrees/certificates offered: Modern Recording Techniques 1, 12 weeks; Modern Recording Techniques 2, 15 weeks; CRT (computer based recording), 10-12 weeks

Tufts University
Medford, MA 02155
(617) 627-3395
www.tufts.edu
Degrees/certificates offered: Interdisciplinary studies in multimedia arts

UCLA Extension Department of Entertainment Studies
10995 Le Conte Ave. Room 437
Los Angeles, CA 90024
(310) 825-9064
www.uclaextension.edu/entertainmentstudies
Degrees/certificates offered: Certificate in Music Business, Songwriting Certificate, Certificate in Recording Engineering, Film Scoring Certificate

Unity Gain Recording Institute
1953 Ricardo Ave.
Fort Myers, FL 33901
(239) 332-4246
www.unitygain.com
Degrees/certificates offered: Certificate of graduation upon completion of each 48-week program

University of Cincinnati
Conservatory of Music (CCM)
P.O. Box 210096
Cincinnati, OH 45221-0096
(513) 556-5462
www.uc.edu
Degrees/certificates offered: Bachelor of Fine Arts in Theater Design and Production; Master of Fine Arts in Theater Sound Design

University of Colorado, Denver
Campus Box 162
P.O. Box 173364
Denver, CO 80217-3364
(303) 556-2727
www.cudenver.edu/cam
Degrees/certificates offered: Master of Science in Recording Arts, Bachelor of Science in Music (major in Recording Arts or Music Industry Studies)

University of Hartford—The Hartt School
200 Bloomfield Ave.
West Hartford, CT 06117
(860) 768-4465
uhaweb.hartford.edu/musicprod
Degrees/certificates offered: Bachelor of Music, Music Production and Technology

University of Hartford—Ward College
200 Bloomfied Ave.
West Hartford, CT 06117
(800) 766-4024
uhaweb.hartford.edu/wardweb/descaud.htm
Degrees/certificates offered: Bachelor of Science in Audio Engineering Technology

University of Maine at Augusta
46 University Dr.
Augusta, ME 04330
(207) 621-3267
www.uma.maine.edu/academics/ucadjazz&contemporarymusic.html
Degrees/certificates offered: Bachelor of Music in Jazz and Contemporary Music (audio concentration)

University of Massachusetts-Lowell
Sound Recording Technology
One University Ave.
Lowell, MA 01854
(978) 934-3850
www.uml.edu/dept/music/srt
Degrees/certificates offered: Bachelor of Music in Sound Recording Technology

University of Memphis
Music Industry Program
106 Communication Fine Arts Building
Memphis, TN 38152
(901) 678-2559
http://memphis.music.edu
Degrees/certificates offered: Bachelor of Music in Music Industry with concentrations in Recording Technology, Music Business

University of Miami
School of Music
P.O. Box 248165
Coral Gables, FL 33124
(305) 284-2241
www.music.miami.edu
Degrees/certificates offered: Bachelor of Music in Music Engineering with either a minor in Electrical Engineering or a double major in Computer Science; Master of Science in Music Engineering

University of Michigan
School of Music
Dept. of Performing Arts Technology
1100 Baits Dr.
Ann Arbor, MI 48109-2085
(734) 763-7558
www.music.umich.edu/departments/pat/index.lasso
Degrees/certificates offered: Bachelor of Music in Music and Technology; Bachelor of Fine Arts in Performing Arts Technology: Music Concentration; Bachelor of Fine Arts in Performing Arts Technology: Media Arts Concentration (Sonic Arts, Visual Arts, Engineering); Bachelor of Science in Sound Engineering; Master of Arts in Media Arts

University of Missouri, Kansas City
4949 Cherry St.
Kansas City, MO 64110
(816) 235-2964
www.umkc.edu
Degrees/certificates offered: Master of Fine Arts in Theater Sound Design

University of Nebraska, Lincoln
206 Avery Hall
Lincoln, NE 68588-0511
(402) 472-2258
www.unl.edu
Degrees/certificates offered: Bachelor of Journalism degree in Broadcasting

University of New Haven
300 Orange Ave.
West Haven, CT 06516
(203) 932-7101
www.newhaven.edu
Degrees Offered/Certificates: Bachelor of Arts in Music, Bachelor of Arts in Music and Sound Recording, Bachelor of Science in Music and Sound Recording, Bachelor of Arts in Music Industry

University of North Carolina at Asheville
Music Department
One University Heights
024 Lipinsky Hall, CPO #2290
Asheville, NC 28804
(828) 251-6432
www.unca.edu/music
Degrees/certificates offered: Bachelor of Science in Music Technology, Bachelor of Arts in Music with a concentration in Jazz Studies, Bachelor of Arts in Music (general music studies)

University of Oregon
School of Music
1225 University of Oregon
Eugene, OR 97403
(541) 346-3761
http://darkwing.uoregon.edu/~fmo
Degrees/certificates offered: Bachelor of Science, Music Technology option; Master of Music in Intermedia Music Technology; and Intermedia Music Technology as a secondary area for doctoral students

University of Southern California
School of Music
Music Industry/Recording Department
Los Angeles, CA 90089-0851
(213) 740-3224
www.usc.edu/schools/music
Degrees/certificates offered: Bachelor of Science in Music Recording, Bachelor of Science in Music Industry, Bachelor of Music in Music Industry

University of Wisconsin at Oshkosh
800 Algoma Blvd.
Oshkosh, WI 54901
(920) 424-4224
www.uwosh.edu
Degrees/certificates offered: Bachelor of Music degree with an emphasis in Recording Technology

Vancouver Film School
200-198 W. Hastings St.
Vancouver, BC V6B 1H2
Canada
(604) 685-5808
www.vfs.com
Degrees/certificates offered: One-year diploma in sound design

Wayne State University Music
1321 Old Main
Detroit, MI 48202
(313) 577-1795
www.music.wayne.edu
Degrees/certificates offered: Undergraduate and graduate degrees in music; program disciplines include music technology

Women's Audio Mission
P.O. Box 410663
San Francisco, CA 94141
(415) 239-3269 x5
www.womensaudiomission.org
Degrees/certificates offered: Audio workshops taught by women for women; audio Certificates are under development

Webster University/Audio Production Program
470 E. Lockwood Ave.
Groves, MO 63119
(314) 968-6924
www.webster.edu/depts/comm/audioprod/audioprod.html
Degrees/certificates offered: Bachelor of Arts degree In Audio Production

Yale School of Drama
P.O. Box 208244
New Haven, CT 06520-8244
(203) 432-8825
www.yale.edu/drama/academics/sound/index.html
Degrees/certificates offered: Three-year Master of Fine Arts in Sound Design; One-Year Sound Engineering Internship

INDUSTRY TRADE MAGAZINES

Audio Media
www.audiomedia.com

Bass Player
www.bassplayer.com

BE Radio
www.beradio.com

Billboard
www.billboard.com

Electronic Musician
www.emusician.com

Entertainment Design
www.entertainmentdesignmag.com

EQ
www.eqmag.com

Guitar Player
www.guitarplayer.com

Guitar World
www.guitarworld.com

Keyboard
www.keyboardmag.com

Live Sound! International
www.livesoundint.com

Millimeter
www.millimeter.com

Mix
www.mixonline.com

Modern Drummer
www.moderndrummer.com

Music Connection
www.musicconnection.com

Performing Songwriter
www.performingsongwriter.com

Post
www.postmagazine.com

Pro Light and Staging News
www.plsn.com

Pro Sound News
www.prosoundnews.com

Recording
http://recordingmag.com

Remix
www.remixmag.com

Sound and Video Contractor
www.svconline.com

Sound on Sound
www.soundonsound.com

Surround Professional
www.surroundpro.com

Tape Op
www.tapeop.com

The Hollywood Reporter
www.hollywoodreporter.com

Variety
www.variety.com

Video Systems
www.videosystems.com

Trade Shows and Industry Events

There are a variety of annual conventions for professionals in the audio field. Below are just a few of the events you may wish to attend. They are listed in calendar order. Check the organization's Website for specific locations and dates.

JANUARY

CES (Consumer Electronics Show)
www.cesweb.org

Winter NAMM (International Music Products Assn.) Show
www.namm.com

FEBRUARY

Grammy® Awards
www.grammy.com

SMPTE (Society of Motion Picture and Television Engineers) Conference
www.smpte.org

MARCH

Winter Music Conference
www.wintermusicconference.com

South by Southwest
www.sxsw.com

NSCA
www.nsca.org

Game Developers Conference
www.gdconf.com

APRIL
NAB (National Association of Broadcasters) Convention
www.nab.org

JUNE
ShowBiz Expo
www.showbizexpo.com

Infocomm North America
www.infocomm.org

JULY
Summer NAMM
www.namm.com

SEPTEMBER
CEDIA
www.cedia.org

OCTOBER
NAB Radio Show
www.nab.org

AES (Audio Engineering Society) Convention
www.aes.org

NOVEMBER
SMPTE Conference
www.smpte.org

SAMPLE LETTERS

Networking Letter: Informal E-mail

Dear Mary,

We met last month at your informative "The New Studio Engineer" presentation at the AES convention; after your lecture, we had a lively exchange about the local job economy. I was inspired by your perspective and came away with some very unconventional career ideas that I'm interested in running by you. I work in Manhattan every Friday and would love to meet up for a coffee if you're free. I'll give you a ring next week to see if we can arrange a good time to get together.

Thanks, and I look forward to speaking with you.

Sincerely,

Leah Smith

Internship Cover Letter

January 11, 2004

5050 Telegraph Avenue
Oakland, CA 94699

Jane Bravo
Video Masters
9999 Wilshire Drive
Los Angeles, CA 90999

Dear Ms. Bravo:

I'm interested in interning at Video Masters. After three years at Audio U., honing my production chops both inside and outside the classroom, I'm eager to dig in and put them to work in the real world. I've been a big fan of Video Masters' post-production work since the famous Space Soda campaign of 1994, and would love the opportunity to volunteer my post skills at your facility. My qualifications make me an excellent fit: I'm fluent in both Final Cut Pro and Adobe Premiere, I've got great PC troubleshooting and maintenance skills, and I make a mean pot of coffee.

I will be in California next month and would like very much to meet with you to discuss ways I can contribute to your facility. I've attached my résumé for your review. I will follow up next week with a phone call to see if I can arrange a time to visit. Thank you in advance for your consideration.

Sincerely,

Thomas Gerber

Thank You Letter

May 23, 2004

19987 Main Street
Beverly, MA 01915

Doug Rock
Music Mania Studios
27984 6th Avenue, Suite 100
New York City, NY 10012

Dear Mr. Rock:

Thank you for taking the time to interview me for your assistant engineer position. I enjoyed our conversation and appreciated the opportunity to gain a deeper understanding of the philosophy and work environment at Music Mania.

Your description of your unique, creative multitasking approach convinced me that I am an ideal fit for your facility: In addition to my certified Pro Tools skills and extensive MIDI programming experience, my campus studio management work demonstrates the organization and attention to detail necessary to excel in a busy, multipurpose music-production environment such as the one at Music Mania.

Thank you again for your consideration, and I look forward to the possibility of working with you.

Sincerely,

Mary Kenny

SAMPLE RÉSUMÉS

ALEX BELL

Current Address:
555 Music Hall
Audio University
New York, NY 10010
(212) 555-1234

Permanent Address:
100 Oak Lane
Berkeley, CA 94699
(510) 555-9876

Email Address and URL:
abell@email.com
http://www.url.com

OBJECTIVE
Internship position in audio post-production at XYZ Post

EDUCATION
B.A. in Sound Design, expected June 2005
Audio University, New York, NY
GPA: 3.6

SKILLS SUMMARY
- Proficient in Pro Tools, AVID, Sonic Solutions, and Cedar audio workstation platforms
- Well-versed in digital and analog audio production techniques, with 300 hours of mixing experience in school studios
- Fluent in C++, JAVA, and HTML programming
- Experienced in project and personnel management, through directing student film, supervising retail employees, and coaching sports teams

AUDIO EXPERIENCE
Senior Multimedia Project
Wrote, directed, and edited "NYCollege Life," a one-hour documentary chronicling college students living in New York City: Auditioned actors, recruited and managed audio and video tech teams, arranged equipment, and supervised location production and post-production, including scoring and mixing original music, and editing dialog and effects

Student Manager, Campus Video Suites, Fall 2001-present
Configured equipment, maintained media inventory, and managed session schedule for two AVID/Pro Tools and two Final Cut Pro editing suites

WORK EXPERIENCE
Assistant Manager, Mountain Wear Co., April 1999 to August 2001
Berkeley, CA
Supervised and scheduled four employees, purchased and managed inventory, implemented 12-weekend outdoor workshop series

Softball Coach, Berkeley Co-Ed League, June 1999-September 2003
Berkeley, CA
Managed five teen league teams, led annual summer training camp

PROFESSIONAL ASSOCIATIONS
AES, NARAS

MEG HERTZ

88511 55th Street
New York, NY 10000

Phone: 212•555•4321
E-mail: address@emailhost.com

OBJECTIVE
To obtain an audio production intern position at Super Studio XYZ

EDUCATION
American Sound Institute, Los Angeles, CA
Audio Master Diploma, May 2003

SKILLS HIGHLIGHTS:
Audio Recording and Production: Completed 900-hour program focusing on audio signal flow and tracking, mixing, and mastering, including nonlinear editing, MIDI sequencing, surround production, remixing, and sound for picture.

Video Production: Learned basic analog and digital video recording techniques, and online and offline workstation editing methods.

Maintenance: Studied electronics and troubleshooting fundamentals, including soldering and tape machine-alignment techniques.

Equipment Proficiency:
Consoles: Neotek Elite, Sony OMXR-100, SSL 9000 J
Workstations: Digidesign Pro Tools, Apple Final Cut Pro, MOTU Digital Performer
Outboard Gear (highlights): Eventide H3000, Lexicon 980L, TC Electronic System 6000, MOTU 1296, Alesis ADAT, Synclavier, Propellerhead Reason, Korg Triton
General Software Applications: Microsoft Word, Excel, and PowerPoint; Filemaker Pro

Gear Certifications:
Digidesign Pro Tools
TC Electronic M3000
SIA Smaart
Antares AutoTune

VOLUNTEER AUDIO EXPERIENCE
Tracked, mixed, and mastered eight-song CD for local rock acts Cage Gods and FleshMetal.
Rented and configured equipment for, mixed, and recorded five-night "Sing-Along Messiah" choral concert series, St. Mark's Parish, Woodland Hills, CA.
Produced "Unamerican Idol" compilation CD: Auditioned and assembled tracks, mastered, sourced graphic design and duplication, developed promotional campaign.

OTHER EXPERIENCE
Waitress, Musso & Frank's, Hollywood, CA	*June 2002-June 2004*
Part-time Telemarketer, Pacific Telephone, Los Angeles, CA	*August 2002-June 2004*
Certified Nursing Assistant, NYC General Hospital, New York, NY	*July 1997-May 2002*

HOBBIES
Write, sing, and play keyboards for New York band Satanface, volunteer piano tutor

INDEX